Technical An
for Beginners

Take $1k to $10k Using Charting and
Stock Trends of the Financial Markets with
Zero Trading Experience Required

A.Z Penn

© **Copyright A.Z Penn 2021 - All rights reserved.**

The content contained within this book may not be reproduced, duplicated or transmitted without direct written permission from the author or the publisher.

Under no circumstances will any blame or legal responsibility be held against the publisher, or author, for any damages, reparation, or monetary loss due to the information contained within this book. Either directly or indirectly. You are responsible for your own choices, actions, and results.

Legal Notice:

This book is copyright protected. This book is only for personal use. You cannot amend, distribute, sell, use, quote or paraphrase any part, or the content within this book, without the consent of the author or publisher.

Disclaimer Notice:

Please note the information contained within this document is for informational purposes only. None of the information herein constitutes an offer to buy or sale any security or trading vehicle, nor does it constitute a trading recommendation of a legal, tax, accounting or trading recommendation by A.Z Penn or paid contributors. The information is presented without regard for individual trading preferences or risk parameters and is general, non-tailored, non-specific information.

By reading this document, the reader agrees that under no circumstances is the author responsible for any losses, direct or indirect, which are incurred as a result of the use of the information contained within this document, including, but not limited to, — errors, omissions, or inaccuracies.

Warning: There is no magic formula to getting rich, in the financial market or otherwise. Trading involves high risk and you can lose a lot of money. Success in trading with the best prospects for price appreciation can only be achieved through proper and rigorous research and analysis. Please do not trade with money you cannot afford to lose. The opinions in this content are just that, opinions of the author. As an author, the opinions, comments, stories, reports, advertisements and articles published are for information and educational purposes only; nothing herein should be considered personalized trading advice. Before you make any trade, check with your trading professional (advisor). We urge readers to review the financial statements and prospectuses of any company they are interested in. We are not responsible for any damages or losses arising from the use of any information herein. Past performance is not a guarantee of future results.

A.Z Penn is 100% independent in that we are not affiliated with any security, trading vehicle, bank or brokerage house.

All registered trademarks are the property of their respective owners.

A huge credit to Andrea Kirkby for her contribution in proofreading and editing the book.

TABLE OF CONTENTS

HOW TO GET THE MOST OUT OF THIS BOOK 8

Introduction 13

Chapter 1: What is Technical Analysis? 17

Chapter 2: Basic Concepts of Trend 32

Chapter 3: Recognising Breakout 51

Chapter 4: The Four Types of Indicators You Need to Know 68

Chapter 5: Continuation Patterns 106

Chapter 6: Reversal Patterns 126

Chapter 7: 16 Candlestick Patterns that Every Trader Should Know 148

Chapter 8: Avoid the Traps 171

Chapter 9: Trading Psychology 186

Chapter 10: Ten Top Tips for Each Aspect of Trading 201

Chapter 11: Designing Your Trading Strategy 211

Conclusion 229

Glossary 240

References 250

Quiz Answers 254

A.Z Penn

HOW TO GET THE MOST OUT OF THIS BOOK

To help you along your trading journey, for this book in particular, I've created a free bonus companion masterclass which includes video analysis of real life stock examples to expand on some of the key topics discussed in this book. I also provide additional resources that will help you get the best possible result.

I highly recommend you sign up now to get the most out of this book. You can do that by visiting the link or scanning the QR code below:

www.az-penn.com

Free bonus #1: Charting Simplified Masterclass ($67 value)

In this 5 part video masterclass you'll be discovering various simple and easy to use strategies on making profitable trades. By showing you real life stock examples of a few charting indicators - you will be able to determine whether a stock is worth trading or not.

Free bonus #2: The Technical Trader Cheatsheet ($12 value)

In this cheatsheet you will be learning the 9 secret lessons that the greatest technical traders taught me. Believe me, when I started out, I thought I had everything set up to make a million on the stock market; but I was definitely in for a surprise.

Free bonus #3: Colored Images - Technical Analysis for Beginners

To keep our books at a reasonable price for you, we print in black & white. But here are all the images in full color.

All of these bonuses are 100% free, with no strings attached. You don't need to provide any personal details except your email address.

To get your bonuses, go to the link or QR code:

www.az-penn.com

Introduction

A lot of people will tell you that "stock trading won't make you money". But you should take a good look at who's saying that. Are they all richer than you? I doubt it. Have they tried trading the markets? Probably not. Do they want you to put your money into a pension scheme, a jatropha farm, an investment fund, a laundrette, or a film financing package instead? I bet quite a few of them do, so they have a vested interest in telling you that trading doesn't pay.

And they're wrong. Stock trading *can* make money if you are disciplined and work hard. That can help you become financially independent. By making intelligent trades, starting small, you can build your portfolio over time and create a platform for even greater future success.

But you need the right tools. You need to be able to take your own decisions, sometimes doing the opposite of the crowd, sometimes taking advantage of the way the money is flowing. And to do that, you need to understand the markets, and how to spot market trends and key change indicators. One of the best ways to do this is by using technical analysis (charts).

A chart simply represents the prices at which shares are being bought and sold. But this gives you a way of analyzing how investors are behaving - if you like, a chart is a kind of shorthand behavioral analysis of the market. As you know from your experience of people at work or at home, if you know how people usually behave, you can usually guess what they're going to do next.

Mum *always* responds to your feeling under the weather by making you your favorite comfort food. So you know, next time you have a headache, that's what she'll do. Stock market behavior is a bit more complex than that, but the essentials are the same; most investors tend to behave in relatively predictable ways. Charts are a way of analyzing that behavior.

If you've already been trading without being able to interpret the information that charts are giving you, or without knowing about these techniques at all, you may have had a very disappointing experience. You may have lost money. You may even be ready to give up.

Or you may have to depend on other traders. You might be using a particular newsletter or subscription service, like Tim Alerts or Superman Trades, or a trading coach. But if you are still following someone else's lead, you're not really independent, mentally or financially. And of course, these services come at a cost, sometimes quite a high cost.

Or you may just be annoyed when you hear other people talking about how "Tesla's just forming a death cross" or "Apple went through a key resistance level today". You have some kind of an idea about what they mean, but you don't really know exactly how it works or how the theory behind it stacks up, and you want to.

I've been there - having someone tell me that the Golden Cross meant I should be buying a share, and wondering what on earth the Golden Cross was and why I should take any notice of it, and being annoyed that I didn't know, and feeling a bit of an idiot. (And I've also been, if not broke, pretty close to the edge. Just so you know.)

That's why I wrote this book. It puts all the information you need about technical analysis - using charts to predict share price movements - in one place, and it puts it in a logical order so that you can take the easy path rather than the steep route up the learning curve.

The going can get tough. Retracement percentages, Bollinger bands, MACDs, oscillation ranges - the language isn't exactly user-friendly. So the book is divided into bite-sized sections that are easy to get through. If you come across any difficult words, there's a whole glossary section at the end. If you need to read a chapter a couple of times to take it all in, that's fine. That will give you a good grounding in the basic concepts before you take on the next chapter.

And there will be a little quiz at the end of each chapter (answers on page 239) so that you can see whether you've taken the concepts well on board, or whether you might benefit from re-reading the chapter or looking at some real-life charts to see if you can trace the patterns.

This book will take you from complete beginner to knowledge of the most advanced charting techniques. Only experience of using them, though, will make you a true master of trading, so I've included plenty of real-world examples for you to practice on. As you start applying the principles to the market in real-time, you'll see how they work, and you'll gain in confidence.

I hope, thanks to this book, that you'll be able to avoid learning the hard way - that's the way I did it. I thought having qualifications in accounting & finance was enough to make money trading - it wasn't. I made mistakes because I didn't know the basics of charting; I messed up because I didn't recognize some of the traps that the stock market lays for investors (that's why there's a whole chapter on avoiding the traps); I made mistakes because I didn't have enough confidence to trust the signals that the charts were showing me.

They say you learn from your mistakes. I certainly did! And what I learned was to go back and make sure I really understood technical analysis, how it works, why it works, and how to use it to make good trades and quickly get out of loss-making positions.

If you've bought this book, you've just made your first step on the way to successful stock trading. I won't lie, it's not going to be easy. It will be tough to learn everything you need to know. There will be days when things go wrong. But if you persevere, you'll develop your expertise, you'll become more confident, and you'll find that soon, it's making a difference to your trading.

If it makes a difference to your trading, it will also make a difference to your life. You'll be making extra money - whether that's to get yourself on a solid financial footing, or to afford a few luxuries. And you'll have a skill that you can be proud of.

And now, let's get started.

1

Chapter 1: What is Technical Analysis?

Technical Analysis is a way of looking at securities price data and using it to predict the probable future performance of that security. Let's say 'security' because you could use it for the stock market, to trade individual shares, or to trade a market ETF. But you could also use it for futures on commodities, for bonds, or currencies, or even for cryptocurrencies. (However, in this book, I'm going to talk mainly about the stock market, because that's the market I know best, and it's probably the best place to get started.)

Securities price data can be made into different kinds of charts - graphically representing the movement of prices. That's a representation of market behavior - that is, what the thousands of people involved in the stock market, from managers of huge pension funds to market traders and retail investors, have been thinking and doing. We know that people behave in certain ways, and that affects the supply and demand of stock.

Statistically, for instance, most people who invested in a stock at $52, if it falls, will hold onto it. They want their $52 back again. So if the stock does get back to that level, they'll sell it. (It's actually dumb investor behavior, but it's very common behavior.) Technical analysis relies on that predictability to analyze common patterns and suggest how they may play out in the future.

While technical analysis could involve running algorithms for a trading program, usually it's approached by drawing and analyzing charts, and that's what I'm going to teach you in this book.

What Technical Analysis Isn't

Technical Analysis isn't a substitute for having a brain and using it. It is not a 100% guaranteed method of spotting profitable situations. It is a *probability* indicator. It will tell you that a stock is *likely* to go up, and may even suggest how much. It will warn you that the market might be topping out, but it will not deliver a certainty that it will do so.

Technical Analysis (let's just abbreviate that to TA as we continue) also doesn't look at what a stock actually does. It will give you the same answer whether you're looking at Coca-Cola shares, Barclays Bank, the Dow Jones Industrial Index, the Brent oil price or a South Korean government bond. It takes no account of credit quality, news, earnings, valuation or any other 'real world' data - all of which can be called 'fundamental analysis' and is a completely different universe.

Technical and Fundamental Analysis are two different schools. However, they're not mutually exclusive. For instance, if you are risk-averse, you might decide you will only trade large shares, do not have excessive debt, and are in mature markets. Some fundamental investors use TA to try to find the best entry point for their stocks, and to spot potential problems arising.

If you're a technical trader, you also do need to be aware of the news affecting any security you're trading. But for the most part, using a TA approach, you don't need to have a view on whether Intel has fallen too far behind the semiconductor market to reverse its market share decline, or whether KFC really does cook the best Popcorn Chicken Nuggets in the world. You'll get a chart signal and you'll trade the shares and that's all you need to know.

Why You Need to Learn Technical Analysis

When I started, I had a good friend who was a little further along the road than me, and occasionally Saj would give me a tip. Sometimes I did pretty well out of his tips. That gave me a false sense of confidence.

Then one day he gave me a tip that looked great. It was a classic chart pattern, that should have been a great breakout. I bought. And I thought it was great, it was the start of an uptrend that would keep going.

Well, I just didn't know quite enough. It did do well. The stock broke out of the trading range and started going up - just what it was supposed to do.

It wasn't Saj's fault. He was away on some training week in Manchester and probably wasn't checking the market all that often, and I was pretty busy that week - we both had day jobs, after all - and for whatever reason, we just didn't connect. But there was a warning signal that the breakout wasn't going to last. This won't mean anything to you right now, but the price hit a resistance level and failed to break through, then it retested it and failed again. That's a classic warning - your fun is over, time to close the trade.

When I looked at the stock market the next morning, half my profits had disappeared already. I couldn't get hold of Saj, I didn't know what to do, and I watched like a rabbit in headlights as the stock kept going down. In the end, I panicked and dumped the stock - and I'm glad I did, because it kept going down. I was lucky; I managed to get out with a small profit. It could have been much worse.

The moral of that story is that following someone else is not going to get you the returns you want. You have to do the work yourself. That's why you shouldn't buy someone else's stock chart newsletter, follow a blogger, or follow tips in the press. Following a guru, even a good one, and an honest one (as some aren't), is never safe. You need to do the work yourself and understand what you're doing.

The Origins of Technical Analysis

TA isn't new. In Japan, traders in the rice market back in the eighteenth century developed their own way of graphically representing the price movement in the market. That gave us what we now call candlestick charts. And they are still being used today, because they show human behavior based on the sentiments of greed, fear, caution or opportunism, and while a lot has changed in a few centuries, basic human behavior hasn't changed at all.

In 19th century America, Charles Dow (yes, that *is* the same Dow as in 'Dow Jones' - he was a co-founder of the Wall Street Journal, too) worked on a theory of price movement and developed various ways of using this to predict future prices. His ideas were further developed in the 1920s to 1940s culminating in the 1948 publication of Edwards & Magee's *Technical Analysis of Stock Trends*, the founding text of the discipline.

In a pre-computer world, technical analysts drew their own charts every day. I'm not old enough to remember that world, thank goodness, but a friend of my father's told me that when he started working in the London Stock Exchange back in the 1980s, one of the partners of the firm still spent the first half an hour of the day putting the latest prices into his chart book and making a note of any patterns that suggested a trade. The chart book was almost as big as his desk - there was just room left for his yard-long ruler, his black, red, blue and green pencils and an old-fashioned wind-it-up pencil sharpener.

Then came the days of very expensive computer graphics services, and now of course you can get immensely powerful charting software if you just pick the right broker. The great days of free charting sites unfortunately are over, except for very basic price charts - your best bet for good free stuff is Bigcharts.com - but there are a few good sites like Stockcharts.com which charge modest monthly fees (and, most importantly, give you a free trial).

TA has kept developing over the years. In the 1980s, western traders discovered candlestick charts, for instance, and a more recent import from Japan has been Ichimoku. I can't help thinking that Ichimoku 'cloud' charting arriving at the same time as cloud computing is more than just a coincidence!

Emphases also change with time. For instance, in some decades it's been trendedness that was the main focus of technical analysts, while at other times it's been breakouts and other discontinuous behavior. However, TA has never been out of fashion.

Just to add, if you're serious about Technical Analysis, you'll want to find some good sources of charts. I like finviz.com, which lets you ask for 'good channels' or 'rising wedges' (particular chart patterns) as well as for stocks by ticker; Stockcharts.com, which has a premium level offering extended facilities; and Bigcharts.com. But many brokers also have good packages - I hear good things about TD Ameritrade's thinkorswim platform, for instance.

We've shown charts from quite a few sources in this book so that you can get used to seeing the way you'll get the information presented on the screen.

The Pros and Cons of Technical Analysis

TA isn't for everyone, and nor is trading. There are many 'buy and hold' investors who aren't fans of TA and trading. They follow gurus like Peter Lynch and Warren Buffett, who say 'buy great companies at a good price' and just hold on for the ride. (In fact, if they used TA, they might be able to buy their shares more cheaply in the first place.) And TA indeed has its pros and cons.

Let's take a look at some of the pros first...
- You do not need a deep understanding of what the companies do, or how their products compare to their rivals'.
- You don't need to be able to read a balance sheet or spend ages poring through annual reports and note 24 to the accounts, section iii.

- If you are a very visual person, charting is really going to suit you because it summarises stock market behavior in a very visual way which you'll find easy to understand.
- Many TA patterns have a high probability (e.g., 70% chance of being right). That beats monkeys throwing darts at the share price pages of the Financial Times, right?
- TA is more suited to short-term trading than fundamental analysis. Fundamental analysis is more suited to a longer-term approach.
- Research shows that if you bought the stock market, over time you'd make a return of about 8% a year by just buying and holding. But if you traded in and out of the market using TA to buy at or near lows, and sell at or near highs, and got 70% of your trades right, then you could double that return.
- If you trade actively using TA, using a good trading discipline, you could increase your initial stake significantly in a short time. Let's face it, it's much easier to become a millionaire at an 8% a year return if you already have $500,000 to invest!

Some of the cons?

- Because TA looks so easy, you can con yourself that you know how to do it without really having understood the principles. It's very easy to *think* you see a pattern that's not actually there. That's why you need to paper trade before you put real money in the market.
- Because TA misses out on all the fundamental information, you might be buying trash. Buying the bounce could be a bad trade if the company goes bust before you can exit! And 'real world' news events could trash a good trade.
- Some TA indicators have a built-in lag. So you may get into a trade a little bit late or out a bit too late.
- TA doesn't work for securities that are illiquid and don't trade frequently. If you think about it, infrequent trading doesn't give you a big enough statistical sample of traders and investors for the signals to be valid.

- 'Buy and hold' actually isn't a bad way for investors who have a busy (and profitable) day job and want somewhere to make a return by investing their surplus funds for the long term without having to do a lot of work. If you don't have the time to devote to doing analysis and trading, and have a good day job, TA might add a little to your returns, but trading is not for you.

Don't forget, fundamental and technical analysis are not mutually exclusive. Some traders who usually trade on gut feel and instinct - and do very well at it - still use TA to refine their thoughts on exactly when to enter and exit a trade.

And also don't forget that whenever we're talking about TA, we're talking about *probabilities* and not certainties. There is no 100% certainty in trading, except that if you make money… you'll have to pay tax on it. (Yeah. Tough!)

A Little Bit of Philosophy

You may have heard of 'random walk' and the 'efficient market theory'. The first says that price changes are random. The second says that at any point in time, the market knows everything that can possibly be known about a stock, so the price reflects that. Both these academic theories would make TA impossible. However, as one City trader once said to me, "That's why those guys are academics and I'm a trader - and I'm the one making all the money!"

In fact, even random events are subject to statistical norms. For instance, if you toss a coin 100 times, you may not be able to predict any single coin toss, but unless someone's cheating, you'll end up with results somewhere between 48 heads and 52 tails and the reverse, even if not exactly 50/50. TA looks at statistical norms and anomalies. And if you introduce humans and a certain load of facts into the bargain, stock markets are never going to be completely random, if only because human emotions are involved.

At the same time, Efficient Market Theory seems to be disproved just about every time there's a profit warning from a big company. Everything that's known might be known - but people will take different views of it. With TA, we're not looking at everything known about the stock, but about how different people are acting on that knowledge.

Let's go a little bit further. The existing price charts are part of the existing knowledge in the market about that stock. So are price patterns like trendlines and breakouts. And yet... trading breakouts still works the majority of the time! Indeed, some writers think that because people use trendlines, target levels and breakouts, many of these prophecies are self-fulfilling.

So it's in my interest to write this book, because the more of you are using these tried and tested TA techniques, the better they're going to work!

Anyway, that was a bit of philosophy, but I think the trader was right. We are going to be empirical - that is, we're going to see *what works* and how to increase the probability that you're getting the right signals from the market. So no more philosophy. Let's take a look at the kind of charts you're going to be using.

Note for paperback readers: You'll be seeing the charts in black and white. It just costs way too much to print them all in color. But you need to see them in color - that's the way you'll be seeing the charts you look at on your computer screen, and if you have three moving averages, for instance, you need to be able to tell which is which.

Therefore, I would recommend you please go to my website: www.az-penn.com and enter your best email address that I should send the colored images document to.

Some Examples of Charts

If you haven't seen anything other than a normal stock market price chart before, let's open your eyes to the kind of extras you're going to see.

To get started with, here's a Google Finance chart. It just shows the price. (There's quite a funny story that goes with it - if you typed 'sell' into Google, it showed the Apple share price. Once it was brought to Google's attention, it somehow stopped working.) Time runs along the bottom axis, and the vertical axis shows the dollar price. Simple. And... not all *that* useful. Generally, it will simply show you the price at each point in time - each minute, each hour, or the closing price each day. That's it.

Now let's look at how a technical analyst might draw lines on a price chart like that one. This one below is what the old guy with the four pencils and the ruler spent his time doing. It looks pretty rough, right? It's not very easy to read, it uses a slightly different charting method than we use nowadays, and it goes back to 1974, when computers were huge things that filled a couple of rooms and used punch cards, and only NASA and the Tax Department could afford them.

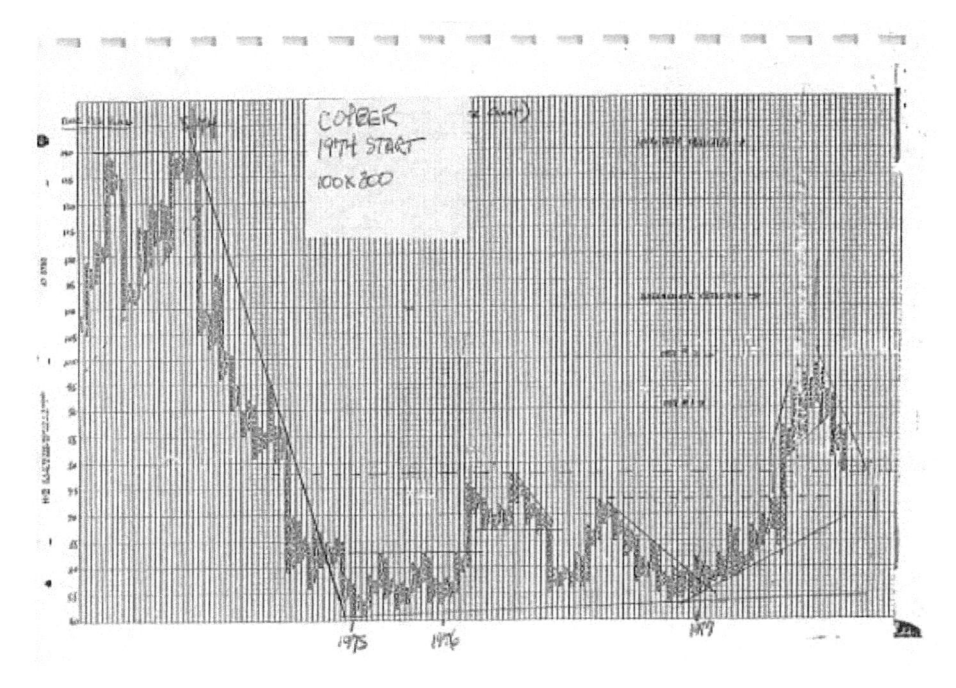

But we still draw trendlines the same way! Drawing trendlines is an art, not a science - it's how your individual gut feel and your experience as you learn more about TA will help you - but the idea is to get a line that summarizes price performance, so that when the share price crosses that line you can see the trend has changed. That breakout is a signal for action. As you can see here, the results were quite dramatic!

As well as drawing trendlines, nowadays computing power allows us to draw other indicators such as moving averages (the average of the last x days' trading), Bollinger bands (a representation of the volatility of a stock, that is, how much prices vary on a given day), and other more powerful indicators.

But using the market price to summarise a whole day's trading behavior is like asking someone what they did at the office today, and them answering 'work'. It's not really all that descriptive. So a slightly more complex charting method shows a bit more. OHLC - Open, High, Low, Close - shows you a bit more information. You get a series of vertical lines, one for each trading day. The vertical line shows you the total range of prices traded, so you can get an idea of whether the market was all over the place or whether the prices were all in a pretty tight range. The little flag on the left is the open and the little flag on the right is the close.

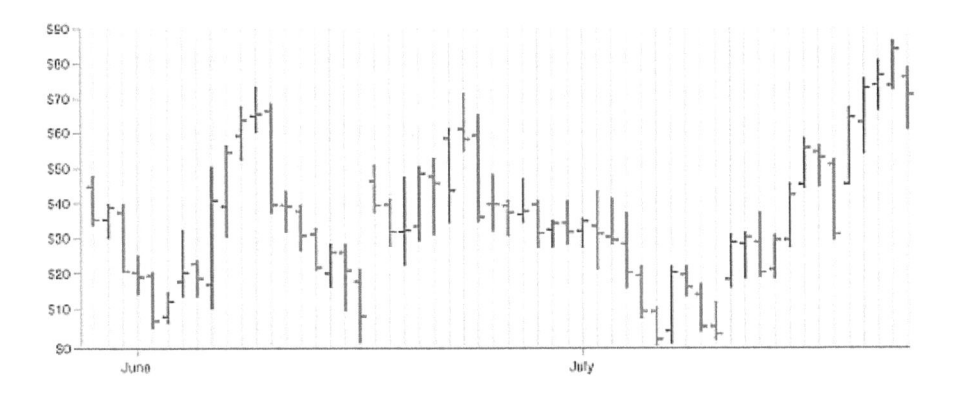

In the chart above, look at the second line. It's small, so prices were pretty close to each other. The left hand flag is lower than the right hand so we know the price closed (right) higher than it opened - that's also why the line is colored green. Then look at the next line. Red - it opened and then fell, and look, the close line is right at the bottom of the range. It's quite a big range. That must have been a dramatic day's trading! So you get a lot more feel for the market out of this OHLC chart than you did just out of a simple daily closing price chart.

As well as capturing prices, TA can show us other information, and it can perform statistical interpretation of price movement. For instance, volume charts show how much stock was traded each day. If I told you that the big change in the ninth bar of the chart - that huge leap up - happened on a day when millions of shares were traded, would you take it more seriously than if only a few thousand shares changed hands? Definitely, a movement that happens with lots of volume is a movement that lots of people participated in - so you'd be right to take it more seriously.

Computers can also subject prices to manipulation, creating a momentum indicator - that is, how fast prices are going up or down and whether that movement is accelerating or decelerating.

And now for something completely different - the next picture shows you a candlestick chart, displayed on a screen with another indicator below it. Candlesticks take a bit of getting used to, but they show a lot of information, and they often give very clear signals. Using two indicators together, the way the candlesticks are used with a line chart below them are also very common. For instance, some chartists put a lot of faith in using two moving averages and noting any place that they cross as a price signal. Or the second indicator might be used as confirmation - for instance, if there's a signal in the candlestick chart, you can use a volume indicator to check that it's 'real' (i.e., that it has a high probability).

At this stage you may be looking at these charts and thinking, "Hey! Let's get started!" or you may have your head in your hands and be thinking, "I'm never going to learn all this." Well, everyone starts somewhere. And one of the reasons I wrote this book is that there is a huge information overload out there on the internet right now. Some of the information is good, some is so-so, and some is downright awful, and if you get started without knowing the basics, then one of two things will happen; you'll find out which is the good information the hard way, or you'll give up before you do.

So we are going to take things gently, we are going to take things systematically, starting with the easiest stuff and going on to more advanced techniques, and I'm going to keep us organized and focused.

Chapter 1 Quiz

1. Why does technical analysis work?
    a) Because mathematical formulas are built into the stock market.
    b) Because charts represent human behavior, which is predictable.
    c) Because share prices obey natural rules like the tides or seasons.

2. Which of these is not a kind of chart?
    a) Candlestick
    b) OHLC
    c) CCTV

3. What is the difference between fundamental analysis and technical analysis?
    a) One is only for traders, the other for investors.
    b) One is about a company as a biz, the other looks only at the share price.
    c) One is easy, the other is difficult.

4. You can learn everything you need to about technical analysis on the internet.
    a) Probably, but it will be more costly and very frustrating.
    b) Yes, of course, it's all out there and easy to find.
    c) What's the internet?

5. Are you going to read chapter 2?
    a) Yes.
    b) Yes.
    c) No, I'd like to watch some paint dry.

Quiz Answers are on page 254

A.Z Penn

2

Chapter 2: Basic Concepts of Trend

What is a Trend

Traders often say, "The Trend is Your Friend." If a given trend has become established, you can piggyback it in whatever direction it's going. And generally, traders only trade *with* the trend. So if a trend is going up, you only trade bounces, and if it's going down, you'll generally trade it by going short (that is, selling stock to take advantage of the dips). The idea is that even if you don't execute your trade particularly well, the trend will help you out and usually ensure you don't make a thumping loss.

A trend is quite simply a direction of price movement. For instance, prices may be trending upwards. That doesn't mean you'll get a price rise every day, but it means that the price will tend to rise over time. For instance, in an upwards trend, you might have closing prices for a bit more than a couple of weeks that went something like; 50, 52, 51, 51, 54, 53, 56, 56, 57, 56, 59, 60, 59. You can see that sometimes prices are up, flat, or even down, but they are moving up on the whole. That's a trend - a general direction. There will be oscillations within the trend, but the trend itself remains unchanged.

That means that you can trade these oscillations within the trend; as long as the trend continues, if you buy when prices are trading lower than the trendline, and sell when they're above the trendline, you'll make money. Trend trading strategies are very common and can be nicely profitable.

Trends often reflect a certain market sentiment - that is, if investors feel the economy is doing well, earnings are going up, the future will deliver better earnings still, there will probably also be an uptrend. But trust what you see on the chart, *not* what you see in the newspapers or on the bulletin boards.

I also need to give you a warning. Traders also sometimes say, "Is it a trend or will it bend?" That's why in technical analysis we need to be able to recognize trends, but we also need to be able to recognize signals telling us that trends are about to end or even reverse. (These are breakouts, and we'll talk about them in the next chapter. But for now, let's go with the flow and stick with the trend.)

Trend has Three Directions

Okay, this is pretty simple. In the words of "those magnificent men in their flying machines," there are three directions:
- UP
- DOWN and
- Flying around - or what traders call 'sideways'.

If you know the lyrics of the song, UP and DOWN are exciting - UP-tiddly-up-up and DOWN-tiddly-down-down - and the 'flying around' or sideways bit is not really emphasized. It's the same on the stock market. UP and DOWN will make you money. They're good strong trends. Sideways, also known as 'ranging' or 'consolidation', can be a big problem, and a market with a sideways trend is hard to make profits in. (On the other hand, when you get a breakout from a sideways trend, you'll notice!)

You'll see many times throughout the book some of my handout slides - yes, they're all drawn with my interactive whiteboard pen, but the good thing about the slides is that I've removed all the distractions that you get on a regular share price chart. No dates, prices, moving average lines, volume bars, whatever - just the trend!

A proper uptrend has increasing highs, but it also has increasing lows. And while a downtrend will hit ever-increasing lows, it should also see each bounce achieving a lower and lower level. Sideways, on the other hand, price movement can be anywhere - sometimes within a really tight range, sometimes just looking chaotic on the chart with prices all over the place.

Technical analysis can help you identify trends and give you good reliable signals when a trend is coming to an end.

Trend has Three Classifications

As well as three directions, the trend has three classifications, or time zones:
- Short term - less than three weeks
- Medium term - a few months
- Long term - six months to a year.

Each market has its typical way of defining these three-time classifications. Futures markets such as commodities futures tend to have shorter timescales, and equity investors have longer timescales, but you'll get the feel of whichever market you trade after a while.

A short term trend can be part of a medium term trend, and a medium term trend can be part of a long term trend - in other words, trends can come nested inside each other. Within a long term bull market (a market in a long term uptrend), for instance, the S&P may have shorter term uptrends separated by short term downtrends - rallies and dips. A longer term investor who is a less active trader may see a continuing uptrend, where you, as a shorter term trader, can see a pronounced short term downtrend.

You might use different trends as different signals.
- Long term trend: okay, there's a trend here, so this is a stock I want to look at. And it's a long term uptrend, so I will generally be buying stock when I think there's a medium term uptrend.
- Medium term uptrend: this gives me my profit expectation. Suppose we're trading low in the long term trend, I can guess where the stock price should be headed within that trend. For instance, in a long term trend where recent high were around $62, and it looks like if it continues it would get to $65 quite easily, and the price is now $56, I have a $9 a share profit potential (and $6 profit potential if the trend fades).
- Short term uptrend: this gives me my timing. So I've got that medium term trend in mind, but when is the best time to get in? When I see a real short term tick up that says to me this is the right time to initiate that short position.

Some people like to look at super long trends, like the idea of Kondratieff waves and 40-year cycles, but those are outside the scope of this book.

Support and Resistance

The trends we want to look at go up and down, and so do their trendlines. But we can also draw some really important straight lines on the chart, and these are called support and resistance lines.

You'll often see a share price exhibit a particular pattern of nearly getting to a price and then refusing to go any further. It's a bit like watching a child playing at the seaside, running down the beach towards the sea, but as soon as a wave comes, running back up the beach squealing happily so her toes don't get wet. Share prices behave just the same way!

A share price might keep falling to a particular price but then rising back again - that's a support line. It's likely that if the share price approaches that line, it will bounce off it again, so this *supports* the price. On the other hand, a share price might keep testing a high, but it never crosses that level - that's a *resistance* line, and the chances are, if it gets to it again, it'll not manage to maintain enough momentum to push its way through.

Here you can see my handouts. I promise you I had not been drinking when I made this one! See how the share prices just touch the resistance and support lines. (A channel has a resistance line at the top and a support level at the bottom - you can make some neat short term trades inside a well-established channel, but the most profitable trades you'll make are on breakouts - which we'll talk about later.)

For instance, look at the way in the chart below. The AT&T share price in the second part of the chart keeps coming up to $29.50 and just falling back again. At the beginning of January 2021, it gets from $28 to $29.25, but it doesn't manage to stay there. Then it gets to $29.75 about 25th January, and then it falls off, then it gets there again about 17th February, and again, it falls off. That's a resistance line, a kind of tidemark. You could put a ruler on the chart and draw it across, and there you have your resistance line.

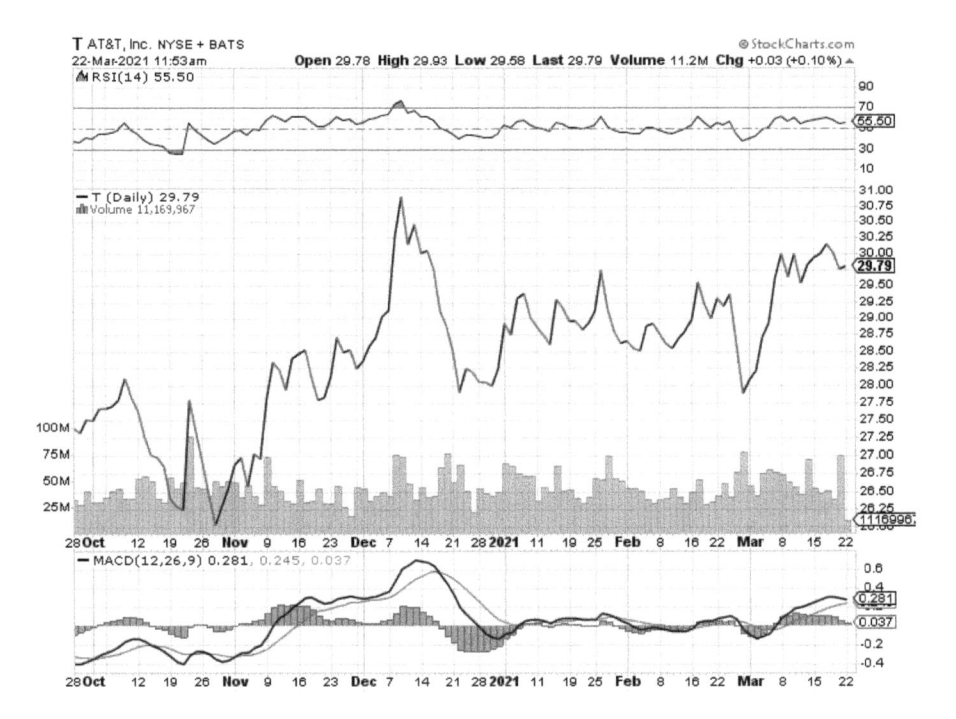

Now the stock has finally managed to push through to $30. It has actually gone through the resistance line… but I'm not sure I'm convinced. I'd want to see another indicator confirming that before I consider it a proper signal. (We'll look at those other indicators in Chapter 4)

But there's another interesting thing; it does look as if the stock has formed a support line, too. Have a go at guessing where it is - and I'm going to give you a clue, again you'll be looking at the more recent half of the time period. Can you draw a straight line which the price approaches, but won't go through? I reckon it's at about $28. Look, it's there just before that bit spikes up, then it falls back to it after the spike, then again at the beginning of March, and every time it bounces.

Now the support line is interesting because it says if I buy at $29, I probably only have a dollar downside, and I know that if the share price goes below $28, then it's time to take that loss and get out.

Why do support and resistance levels work? One reason is 'anchoring', the way that certain information gets stuck in our minds. Investors and traders often remember the price they bought or sold at, and a lot of investors say, "I'm not going to sell till I get my money back". If a lot of them bought at $52 and the price went down temporarily to the mid $40 levels, then when they see $52 again, they'll sell - which by the rules of supply and demand, will cause the price to stop rising. That's a resistance level in action.

The more times a share price unsuccessfully tests a support or resistance line, the stronger that support or resistance becomes. Buying close to support or selling close to resistance makes a good trade, as you'll capitalize on the bounce. But you'll want to put a stop-loss just below a support line (or above resistance) to make sure that if there's a breakthrough, you cut your losses and make a quick exit.

By the way, if a share price does break through a resistance line, that old resistance line will now become a support line. And if a share price breaks through a support line to the downside, that support line will now function as a resistance line preventing the price from rising past it.

Trendlines

It's not always easy to see the market trend. If there's a lot of price movement, you may be able to see that the market's in an uptrend, but not how steep the slope is or how fast prices are rising. You're seeing all the noise, and that makes it difficult to see the signal - the real trend. Drawing trendlines on the chart can help you visualize the trend.

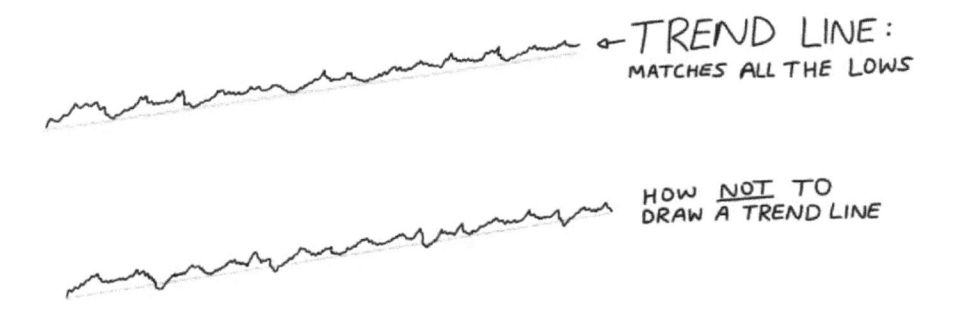

Basically, if the market's in an uptrend, then you're going to try to find a line that it keeps coming back to at the bottom. Find the lowest points that the price hits, and join them up. You are lucky. The software will do it for you - or at least help you do it - whereas this was a pencil-and-ruler job well into the 1980s. So what you should have is a chart that now looks as if all the peaks are 'sitting' on a line of support.

For a market in a downtrend, you're going to do things differently. You're going to draw a line that goes through the highest highs - the places that the price gets to when it bounces, but then runs out of steam and falls back.

Okay, with support and resistance, I showed you my hand-drawn pictures first. This time let's jump right into the real world and look at Amazon. I went on StockCharts and I just couldn't believe what a great example of a channel I'd got, so I stuck it into my drawing software and put in the trendlines - the real trendline is the straight one underneath, that's pushing it upwards, but you can also see there's a straight resistance trendline at the top. (The other two curvy lines are Moving Averages, which we'll cover later on)

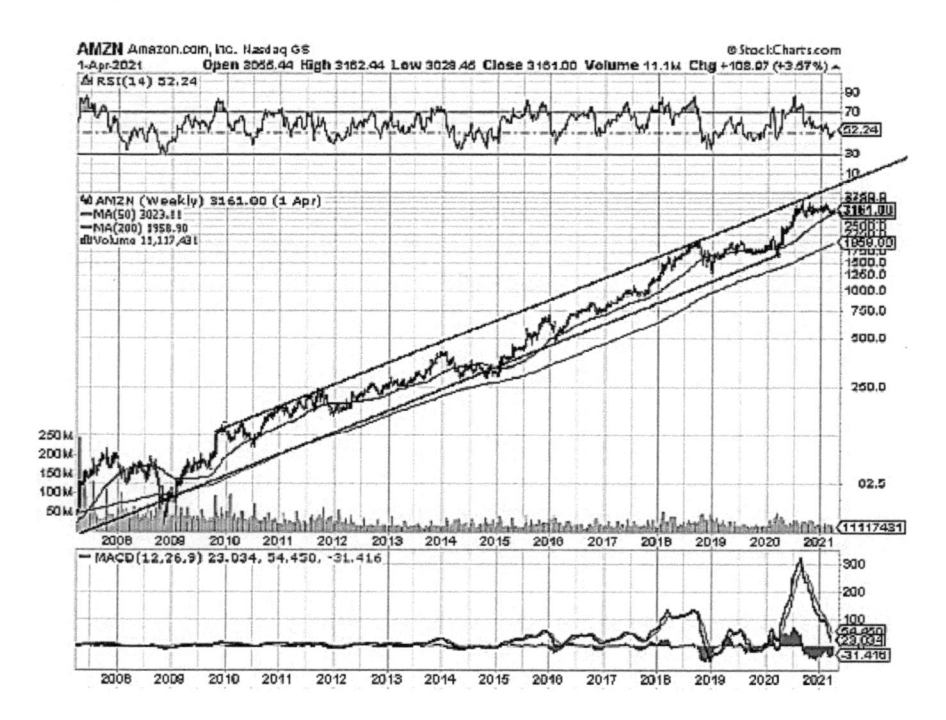

A trendline shows you very clearly the direction in which the market is moving and the speed of the move. It also acts as a support of the resistance line; for instance, in a downtrend, if the price goes towards the trendline (which is above the price bars), then you're getting to a decision point where it will either fall back again, or make a breakthrough.

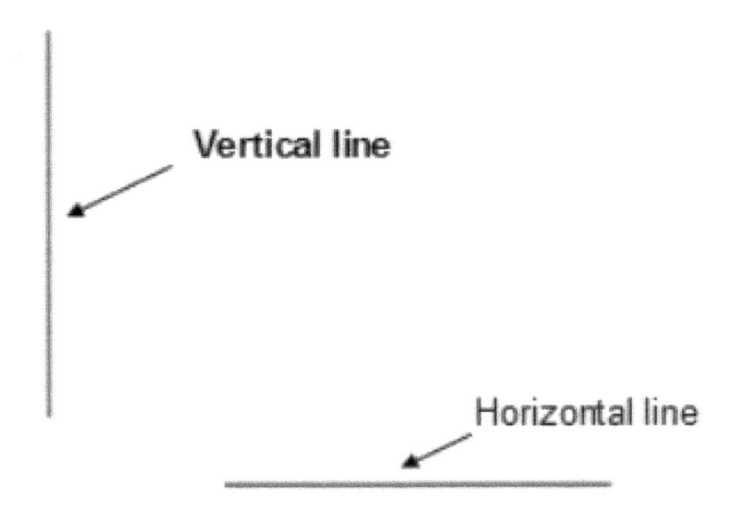

Vertical line

Horizontal line

What you're doing is not very different from drawing support and resistance lines, but you're trying to get a slope instead of a horizontal line. The chart we just looked at is horrible for trying to draw a trendline, although it's got good support and resistance, so let's try something with an uptrend.

Here's Realty Income, where you have quite a lot going on, but I want you to look for one very clear uptrend. Just look at the candlesticks and ignore the other lines on the chart for the moment. They'll be covered in a future chapter. But this is the kind of thing you'll see when you open a charting package - this one comes from StockCharts - and you need to get used to focusing on the lines that matter first, and then to look at the rest. Get some practice by grabbing a straight edge and trying to find the line of best fit - that's the trendline. (The trendline is *not* shown on this chart, you have to draw it yourself – but if you want to see a live visual demonstration on how to draw a trendline correctly, then I would recommend you watch my *free bonus companion masterclass*, as that covers this topic in a lot more detail to help your understanding.)

You see from the dip in the share price in early 2021 (down to 11th January) that it quickly establishes an uptrend, and if you draw a line under the lows, although it heads higher, and then back, it doesn't break the trendline, it keeps bouncing back from it and making higher highs (that is, every little spike goes higher even if it falls back a little in between) all the way through January and the first part of February. Let's assume you got in around $58 in mid-January because you waited a little while to be sure it was a real uptrend; the stock would have gone to $63 (around 14th February) before finally breaking the uptrend by dipping to about $61 towards 18th February. That's $3 a stock profit, or 5% in about a month. You might have done a bit better than that of course, if you didn't wait for the sell signal, but got out nearer to $63 a few days earlier.

One way of thinking of the share price is that it's connected to the trendline by a rubber band. It can get further and further away from the trend, but the stretchy rubber band will generally keep pulling it back. If it hits the trendline, it'll usually bounce. But as it gets close to that trendline, you're going to want to watch out - this is a dangerous time, and it's also, for some traders, an opportunity, as there could be a breakout.

Occasionally you might need to redraw a trendline. It may become steeper or it may, on the other hand, become less steep as price rises decelerate. That doesn't necessarily mean the trend has ended. However, when an uptrend becomes very steep, that could suggest the kind of manic frenzy that often accompanies a market top, so beware of trading in such conditions and keep an eye out for bearish signals (that is, signals telling you the price is going to fall) such as a drop in momentum or moving averages.

Trend Channel

We already saw how if you connect up the highs and the lows, you can create a wide bar with roughly parallel lines, as we did with Amazon. These two lines define the trend channel. I actually like trend channels a lot as a way to trade, but you do need practice in drawing them properly.

There are several things you need to know about trend channels.
- The longer a channel continues, the stronger the trend. (Remember that Amazon trend! Over a decade of it!)
- If a trend channel is combined with a strong trading volume, it's more reliable than if trading is weak.
- If the price breaks out of the channel, it is likely to move quite significantly in the direction it has now established.
- A narrow channel doesn't give you much room for trading - if a stock is always trading within about 2% of the trend, that limits your potential profit. On the other hand, a wide channel, where the stock has some volatility within the overall trend, gives you a chance of larger profits.

If you get a good horizontal channel, running all the way across the page instead of up and down, this is one of the few times it's worth trading a stock that is not in an uptrend or a downtrend. You may have a stock where, for instance, a certain level of dividend yield means income investors tend to buy whenever it comes down to the bottom of the range, and sell when it gets to the top - you don't need to know the reason, just trade the channel. Buy on the bottom of the channel, sell at the top.

Channels are also really useful for setting your stop-losses and profit expectations. If you buy at the bottom, you're looking to exit at the top, but you should also set a stop-loss just below the bottom of the channel. If you've got it wrong, that stops you from being caught by an unexpected breakout.

By the way, you can even sometimes see from a channel how long the share price usually takes to move from bottom to top of the channel. That gives you a good idea of how long your trade will last so you can time it nicely!

Besides simple price channels, there are other kinds of channels, which use volatility rather than price indicators, such as Bollinger bands. But for the moment, let's just stick with the price channel; that's quite enough to get your head around!

Now go and find a few stock charts, and see if you can spot some price channels. See how many times the price bounced around within the channel and work out if you could have made a profit by trading it every time the price touched, or nearly touched, the bottom line.

Divergence

Remember, "is it a trend or will it bend"? Divergence is one way to tell. Now so far, we've talked about the trend, the channel, support and resistance. You can make nice profitable trades by using them as your guide. But sometimes prices break out of their trends.

There are quite a few reasons that might happen. For instance, you sometimes see that if a stock gets promoted to a major market index, and big investment funds and Exchange Traded Funds have to buy the stock because it's in the index. Or a stock might have a profit warning which the market wasn't expecting, and the price goes way below the range. Or a war might break out, or there could be unexpected political news that drives the markets higher or lower. You might also see the end of a big investor exiting their position - for instance, with some IPOs, the end of a lock-in period may see some of the sponsors, founders or management selling out. Or it may happen "for no reason".

Well, the reason is really that every time the trendline was tested before, there were buyers or sellers at the right price to send the stock back up. And this time, there weren't. And if that's the case, that quite likely reflects a slight change in market sentiment, and there are a few ways you could pick that up *before* the breakout. That's where divergence comes in.

When you're looking at your price chart, use a momentum or trading volume indicator (like an oscillator) running beneath it. (We'll take a good look at those and the way they work later - for the moment, don't worry about what they mean, just look at the pictures.)

Usually, you'll see the two lines run pretty much in the same direction most of the time. But if you have an uptrend, and the oscillator is headed downwards, that's a *negative divergence* and it suggests that the uptrend might not continue.

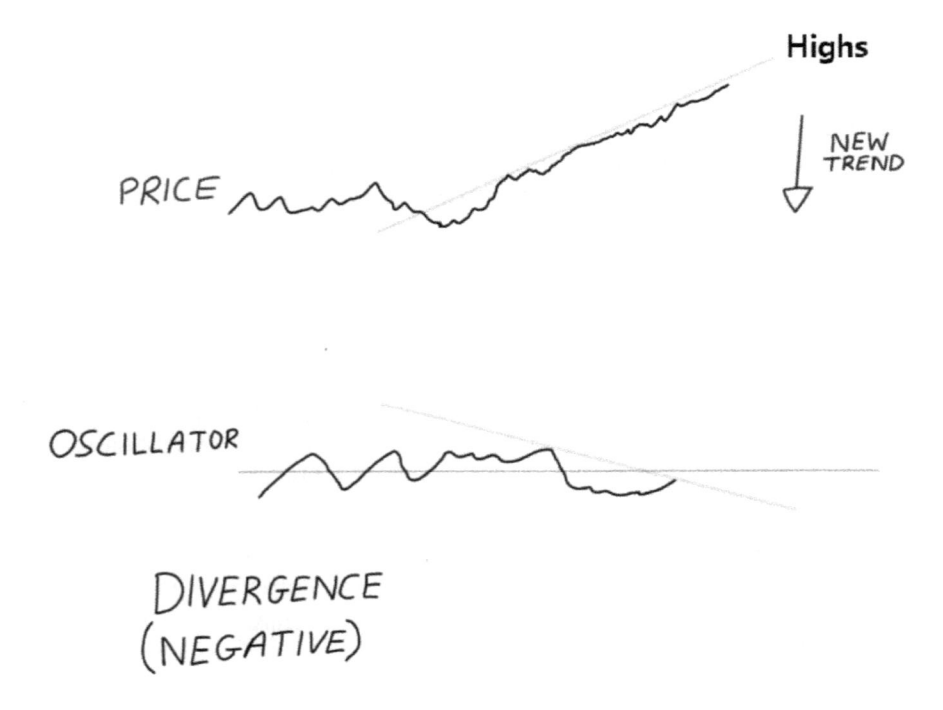

On the other hand, if the price just made a new low, but the momentum indicator is headed up, that suggests prices might rise - *positive divergence*.

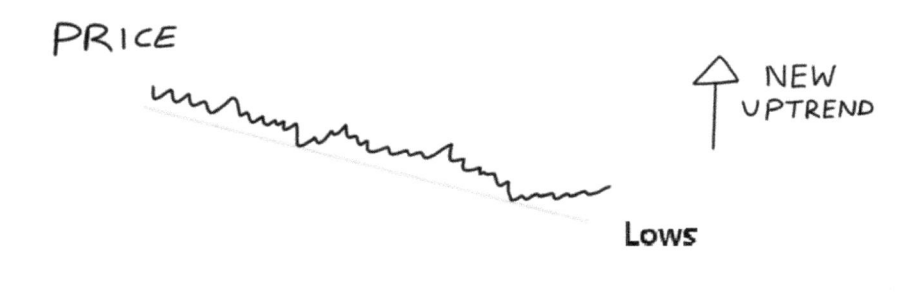

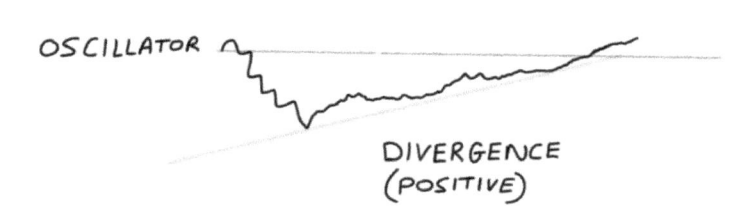

```
PRICE                                    ↑ NEW
    ╲╱╲╱╲╲╱╲╱╲                             UPTREND
              ╲╱╲╱╲╱╲
                      Lows

OSCILLATOR  ╱╲        ╱╲╱╲╱
           ╱  ╲╱╲╱╲╱╲╱
          DIVERGENCE
          (POSITIVE)
```

What you're seeing in the case of negative divergence is that while the price trend looks as if it's continuing, it is decelerating or falling behind the market. So that's an indicator that your price trend isn't as strong as you think it is. But you don't need to pay attention to it all the time - just if:
1. Your price is hitting new highs/lows,
2. Or you think you've got a double top or bottom forming (and we'll talk about those later).

To check if you really have divergence, connect up the highest highs, or lowest lows, and connect up the lines for the indicator for the same period - joining highs to go with price highs and lows to go with price lows. If the slopes are the same, great. If they're moving in opposite directions, you have divergence.

Divergence is not a signal - it doesn't tell you to trade. But it *is* an alert - that is, when you see divergence, if you're risk-averse, it's time to exit your position, and if you're a risk-on kind of person, it's time to stick close to your trading screen and watch that stock like a hawk.

Chapter 2 Quiz

1. The trend is your ....?
   a) Friend
   b) Opposition
   c) Share price

2. How many directions can a trend go in?
   a) Two
   b) Three
   c) Fifteen

3. What can divergence tell you about a trend?
   a) It might not be as strong as it looks
   b) It's going to reverse immediately
   c) Nothing

4. What is a support line?
   a) A horizontal line that shows where share prices have often traded, on a lower level than the share price now
   b) A trendline that shows how fast share prices are going up
   c) Similar to a VPL

5. What is a trend channel?
   a) A channel made by the trendlines that connect tops to tops and bottoms to bottoms, within which the shares trade
   b) Fox News
   c) A sideways trend.

3

Chapter 3: Recognising Breakout

So far we have talked about trading within a range. That can be really profitable and it can also be quite a low risk, low effort form of trading if you identify the right stocks and keep an eye on the patterns.

But if you want to hit the big time, you want the runaway profits that come with a breakout. Remember that "ball on a rubber band" idea I used when I talked about the share price and the trendline? What happens when the rubber band breaks? The ball goes way, way up into the air (or, of course, if we're talking stocks, it could also go in the other direction) - that's a breakout! Compared to trading the range, trading a breakout is like jumping on a train when it's already started moving.

Just so you know: a <u>breakout</u> can happen in either direction, up or down - it's simply breaking out of a pattern.

A <u>breakdown</u>, on the other hand, only goes down.

Breakout

A more technical description of a breakout is that it's when a stock price moves outside an established channel, support or resistance line, with increased volume. (The increased trading volume is required to show that it's a real breakout and not just a fluke.) Breakouts move to the upside, and they move fast.

BREAKOUT

A genuine breakout is a big, bold move. If you're looking at a candlestick chart, you'll see a big bodied candle closing well above the resistance level. If all you see is the price just poking over the edge of the resistance level, that's not a real breakout - it's a fake-out. If you see the price getting near to the resistance line, but it hasn't gone through it yet - it's a fake-out. Wait for the line to be broken before you trade.

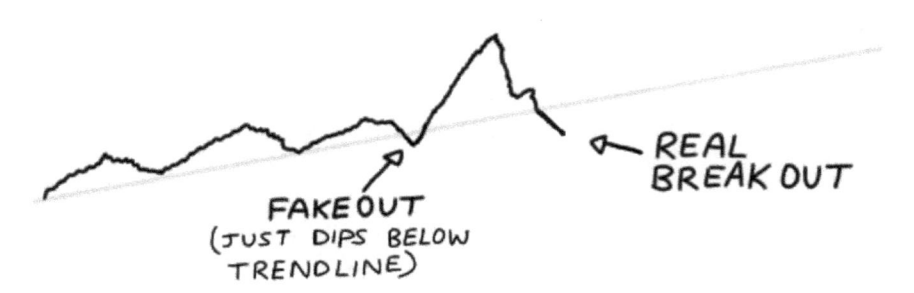

FAKEOUT (JUST DIPS BELOW TRENDLINE)

REAL BREAKOUT

Note by the way that a breakout can happen even in a bear market, that is, a market that is in a major downtrend - there won't be so many breakouts to trade, but stocks that have the strength to move against the market are stocks that should really get going once they start, so you will still get that speedy rise.

Your signal is simple - it's the first time that the price breaks out of the channel, or breaks the resistance line, *and closes above it*.

How do breakouts work? One way they work is what's called a lockout rally. Imagine you have a well-known stock that's had bad results for a couple of years, it's taken a bit of action, and it's stopped going down but it hasn't begun to move up yet.

Everyone is thinking it will soon be time to buy it again, but they haven't bought it yet; they're waiting for something. And for whatever reason you get a little buying - maybe one brave fund manager, maybe a couple of brokers getting in - and it goes through the line, and now all those people who haven't bought it have a massive feeling of FOMO (which, as if you didn't know, means Fear Of Missing Out). It's motoring, so it must be time to buy, so they buy, so it goes up a bit more, so more people buy…

At that point, of course, the short term traders are already getting out with their profits!

How to find breakouts

If you're looking for breakouts, you won't find them. What you're looking for is the pre-breakout pattern. You're looking for stocks that are trading in a fairly narrow channel, that are trading in a really boring way - almost so the candlesticks fill the channel. You're looking for stocks that are range-bound. That is, stocks that are stuck in a range, which keep bouncing from top to bottom and back again without ever going anywhere. This kind of build-up is absolutely classic. It's like a pressure cooker - when it goes, it's going to explode.

You can also look for stocks that are close to their 52 and 26-week highs - this information is easy to find on any finance site. If stocks are trading at a high for the period, they're also going to be close to a resistance level or close to the top of the trendline. That means they'll either be close to a fall back down again into the channel, or they'll be ready to break out. By looking for stocks that are close to a high, you've cut out all the stocks that are not really going anywhere much, so you've reduced the number of charts you need to look at before you find a good breakout pattern emerging.

Of course, you can also look for stocks close to 52 and 26-week lows. That might catch the 'bouncers'.

Draw your resistance lines on the chart - even if they were last hit some time ago - and keep monitoring those stocks every time the price gets towards that resistance line. Use a volume indicator too - the best stocks for a breakout are those that haven't traded in much volume. You're looking for a market where investors have got bored, and they're not doing much - when you get the breakout, that's when they will get interested again! Then you will see the volume accompanying the share price move, which is how you know it's for real.

Another good potential configuration is where you see a resistance level that has been repeatedly tested by sharp spikes. You're looking for the share price to make big spikes, to make a big jump to test the resistance level, and then for it to fall back really steeply. You don't want to see gentle waves; you want to see a spiky mountain landscape of strong rallies that quickly reversed.

Or if you're a beach bum - you want to see big surf, not nice gentle waves. These spiky, punchy price movements show that the resistance level is a good strong one. It's as if the share price took a real run-up, but it still couldn't punch through the wall. So that's a tough wall, and any breakout that makes it through the resistance will be a massive one. The bigger the breakout, the more money you'll make on the trade.

Further good signs that a breakout could be coming are:
- The channel grows narrower
- A build-up period in which prices form a tight cluster
- Trendlines which make an ascending triangle - the lows are getting higher, but the highs have been on the same trendline
- The resistance level has been tested unsuccessfully several times.

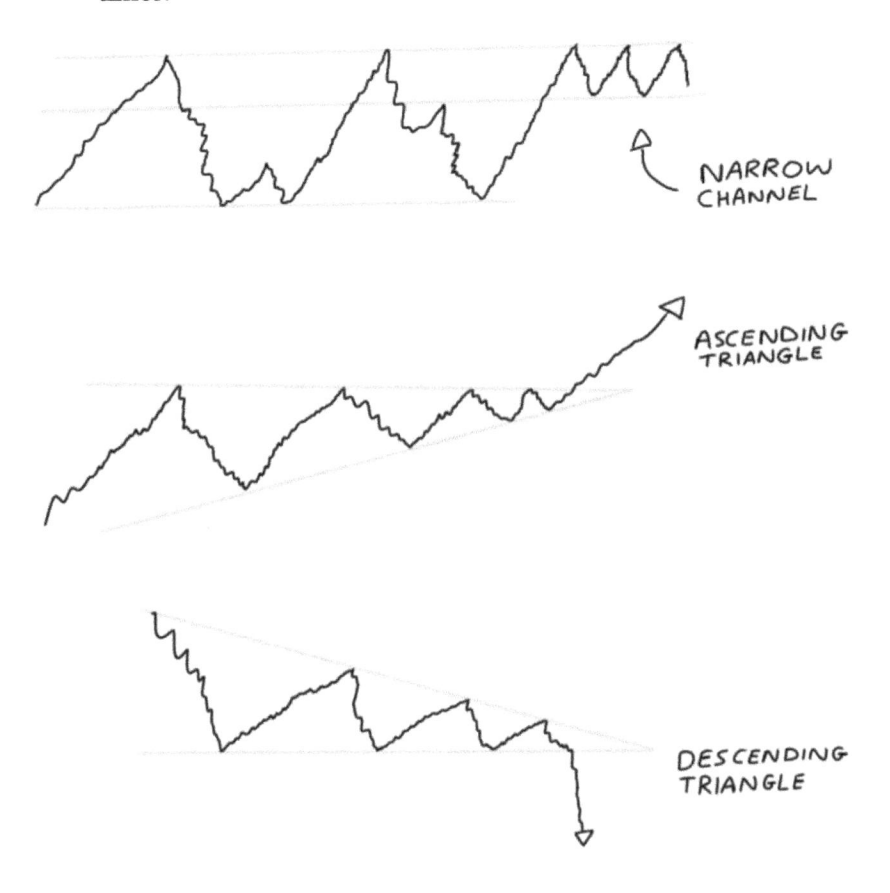

NARROW CHANNEL

ASCENDING TRIANGLE

DESCENDING TRIANGLE

The longer the build-up, the bigger the breakout. Once you've found your targets, plan your trade in detail *before* any breakout. I'm going to talk about trading tips later - but you should always plan your trade so that when the breakout comes, you can act real fast. Remember, breakouts are fast.

What do you do if you miss a breakout? If it was preceded by a really good consolidation period (trading within a limited price range), and has made a definitive move to the upside, you should jump in even though you're a bit late. You'll probably use the techniques you already learned in the chapter on trends to spot the right place to enter your position, as well as to set a good stop-loss. Or if it looks as if it's a pretty small breakout, you could wait for the price to test the line that was the old resistance level, and has now become a support level, and you could buy it then. Happily, you do quite often get a second chance!

Breakdown

What's a breakdown? It's just a breakout, except that the share price goes down instead of up. So it will usually be announced by a descending triangle in some cases - lower highs, but the lows are forming a horizontal line. Like a breakout, it's usually on high volume and will lead to a large price swing, and usually then into a new downtrend. It can often be very quick, which is why you need to set up your trendlines and then monitor them whenever you see a potential breakdown trade setting up.

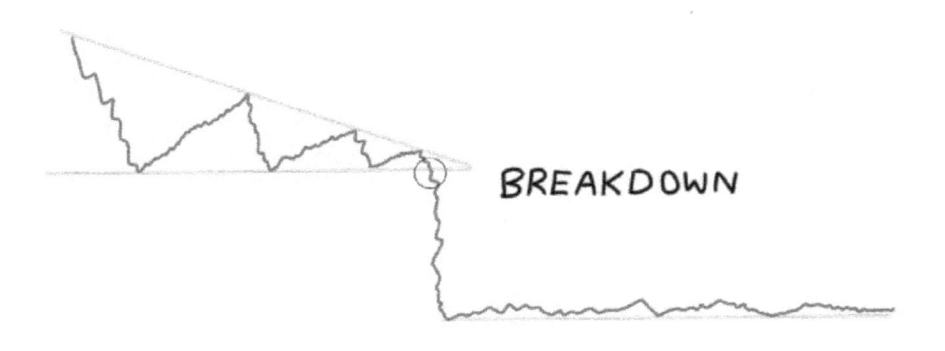

Looking for a breakdown by just looking at loads of charts is like looking for a needle in a haystack. On the other hand, if you have collected half a dozen charts that show tight consolidation build-ups and descending triangle trendlines, you pretty much know one is going to show up - but you have to be ready to act when it does. (That might mean actually watching your screens, but it could also mean setting up stop-limit orders with your broker and just letting them run.)

However, taking advantage of a breakdown isn't as easy as trading a breakout because you need to be able to short trade or trade options. Not everyone is happy trading short. (There's a subsection on this coming up.)

If you do go short, the best way to set up the trade is to put a sell stop-limit-order just below the support level. That is, an order which specifies a price at which the order becomes valid, *and* a price limit after which it is no longer valid (e.g., "Sell 100 IBM *if* the stock price falls below 90 but *not* if it goes below 95.) It's a good way of entering a breakout or breakdown trade. But if there is high volume and a lot of price action, you might not get your order filled. So waiting for a retest (or another chance) of the trendline that has now become a resistance level might give you a better price - *if*, of course, there is a retest. You can never be sure.

As always, decide your exit strategy before you enter the trade. Many traders use the moving average (which we'll talk about in the next chapter) - once the share price closes above the moving average, it's time to quit. (Think about that for a second; the moving average shows the average of prices for the *last* 20 days, let's say. As the share price falls quickly, it will fall *below* the moving average, because the moving average still has all the higher prices from previous trading days in it. As long as the price is still falling quickly, that will continue to be the case, but the moving average will eventually catch up once the fall decelerates. At this point, the stock *might* rebound, but even if it doesn't, the easy gains are gone and you can find a better trade elsewhere. Anyway, we'll talk about this again next chapter when it should make more sense to you.)

Channel Break - some trading tips

Let's look at a typical channel break and see how to trade it. Technical Analysis will give you good trading ideas, but you also need to learn *how* to trade. And if you haven't been involved in the stock market before, or if you've always been a buy and hold investor making simple market buy orders, you have a lot to learn.

First of all, you need to work out your profit target, and this will probably (though not always) also be your exit point. This is something buy and hold investors never bother with. It's easy with a channel break, though; look at the width of the channel, and if it's $6, then add $6 to the price at the resistance line, and that's your immediate profit target. If you're trading a round lot (100 shares), that's a total $600 profit.

Your goal should be to stack the odds in your favor, so usually, I like to see a stop-loss that's half the size of the expected profit if the trade works. In this case, that would be $3. If the stock falls to $3 below the resistance line, you're out. You've lost $300. This seems like a reasonable balance to me, risking $300 against $600 with a good chart formation that has something like a 70% probability.

In fact, let's just multiply the probabilities to see how good it is;
$600 x 70% = $420
$300 x 30% = $90

So if I'm right about that probability, then I have an expected value of $420-$90 = $330. It's positive. But even if the probability was only half - now come on, do the numbers. It's still a good chunky positive number. What we calculated here was what statisticians call the *expected value* of all the probabilities, and you need this number to be a positive one. If it's negative, what you're making is not a trade but a gamble.

Don't just set the trade and run away. Keep monitoring it. In particular, you should be watching the volume indicator - if this is a genuine breakout, then you'll see the sellers coming in and the volume increasing. So you might get to your original exit point, and say that having reconsidered the situation, this looks like a massive breakout. In which case, set a new stop-loss, and you might even decide to scale in, that is, increase your position by buying more shares.

But if you do scale-in, remember to reset your stop-loss. With a breakout into a bullish trend, you may have this setup:
- You entered the position at $70
- Expected profit $6 (using the channel range) = $76 share price
- So the stop-loss is $3 = $70-$3 = $67
- The price quickly gets to $73, you can see a lot of volume in the market, so you decide to scale in. If you keep your stop-loss at $67, your potential extra profit is $3 (from $73 to $76), but your potential loss is now $6 ($73 all the way down to $67). So you need to pull your stop-loss up higher, to say $71, so your expected return is still greater than your possible loss.

Also, remember how we talked about different lengths of a trend? A breakout could just be one breakout in a series. Look at the chart of Mattel above, and you'll see that there are three series of consolidation/build-up phases, tight channels of trading, followed by breakouts. Can you draw the rough trendlines and work out the dates? (C'mon, this is what you're going to be doing every day as a trader.) Okay... Consolidation from late January to the middle of April, then a breakout (or breakdown); more consolidation till the middle of June when there's another breakout; then more consolidation through July, with a bit more volatile price action this time, and then a breakdown just before the beginning of August.

If you're a long-only trader, this chart is no good for you. But if you can go short, whether your broker lets you sell short (and effectively 'lends' you the stock for the meantime), or whether you can take out options, then this is a great chart. It's particularly good because you have these short-term big steps down. Going short costs money, and options have expiry dates - so you're looking for *shorter term* trades as well as simply going short.

The first breakout in mid-April went from $25 to $21, then the second one in June went from about $22 to $20. But the third one in late July started at $21, and the downtrend ran all the way to below $15 by mid-September. The final breakout in mid-November leads to a severe downtrend in December. If you'd made good money on the first breakout, you might have said, "right, I'm done with that stock". You would have been wrong. There were another two good chances to make almost the same profitable trade, and the last was the best.

Hey, what was that gap up in November 2017 though? Apparently, the stock had got so low that there was talk of bigger toy company Hasbro buying it, and the stock jumped - but as you can see from the end of the chart, nothing happened.

The 'gap' by the way is when prices open above the previous day's closing price, with nothing in between. You'll quite often find it relates to corporate news, whether that's a takeover rumor, as here, or an earnings surprise.

Short Selling

If you want to make the most of breakdowns, you're going to need to be happy short selling or using instruments which allow you to replicate a short sale.

Basically, short selling is selling a stock you don't own. It's as if you promised to deliver a new smartphone to a friend of yours, anticipating you can get it at money off on Black Friday. You charge your friends ten percent less than the retail price, you get the phone at 40% off and keep the change (though possibly not your friend). Short selling allows you to make money out of a forecast that a price is going down. If you'd shorted Nasdaq just before the tech crash, you'd have made a huge return, but a lot of traders just take 4-5% on each of their shorts.

The risk, of course, is if you'd sold your friend the smartphone at ten percent below retail, then found out that the version he wants has just had a price rise and isn't in the Black Friday sale, you'd lose money because you'll have to buy it at retail and he's still going to want that 10% off.

Shorting is not that easy to do as a retail investor - institutional investors like big mutual funds, pension funds or hedge funds, and bank trading desks, make more use of it, often for portfolio protection rather than trading purposes. However, there are a few ways you can go short the market.

- If you have a margin account with your broker, and permission to short, your broker will 'lend' you the shares in your margin account and then sell them on the market on your behalf. You will at some point either close the trade at a profit, close it at a loss, or possibly have to pay a margin call to keep your trade going if it's out of the money at the time (which is why you need a tight stop-loss).
- For the market as a whole, or individual sectors, you could buy an inverse ETF (exchange-traded fund). This kind of fund delivers the reverse of the market return, so if the market goes down, the ETF goes up. You buy and sell them just like you buy and sell a share, and they are low-cost funds, so you won't lose a load of entry commissions like you would with a mutual fund. This is my preferred choice if I see a good short trade in the S&P, for instance.
- You can also use options. Frankly, there is a whole lot of very specific knowledge that you need to trade options - for instance, they come with expiry dates, so their value varies according to the time you have left as well as the price of the stock. Unless you are mathematically minded and willing to get to grips with the specifics (and take a look at the Black-Scholes formula if you're tempted), leave them alone.

- Finally, you *could* use something called a Contract for Difference (CFD), unless you're in the US or Hong Kong. However, you may find in other jurisdictions they are only available to certain investors - professionals, high net worth individuals, and those who can display a high level of market expertise. Frankly, I would avoid them till you've got several years of profitable trading behind you. Even then - be careful.

Please let me emphasize that while stop-losses are important for all trading, they are *especially* important if you go short. If you buy a stock at $600 and it falls, the most you can ever lose is $600 a stock. That's it. Wipeout. But your house, your car, your collection of Pokémon cards, none of that's on the line. Nor are your other stock positions. I *have* been completely wiped out on one or two stocks (both, as it happens, involved corporate fraud), but I lived to tell the tale.

On the other hand, how high can a share price go? $100? Higher. $500? Higher. Tesla has been as high as $900. Want more? Berkshire Hathaway trades at $380,482.75. There is, effectively, no limit to how high a share price can go. That means if you go short, there is no limit to the amount you could potentially lose. You could lose your shirt - your house, your savings, the rest of your portfolio, the lot.

So if you go short, make sure you have your trades thought through in advance, including your stop-loss, and don't let anything prevent you from using that stop-loss. That stop-loss could just save your life.

False Breakout

This is the biggest problem with breakout trading - there are simply too many false breakouts. And that's one reason I've emphasized probabilities and stop-losses because not every breakout trade will work, so you need to minimize the impact of the fake-outs. That's in contrast to trading *within* a channel, where your profits will be more limited, but you have a slightly better probability.

This is why you need a good trading strategy - you'll need to maximize your profits *and* make sure that you control any losses very tightly, because the win/lose ratio is probably not going to be as good as with range trading.

One indicator you need to look at is volume, and there's actually one in particular which is useful for breakouts - Volume weighted moving average (VWMA). In the case of a fake breakout, it won't do much at all - in the case of a real breakout; it will accelerate upwards, giving you confirmation that you've made a good trade. VWMA also gives you your exit level, as once the price falls below the VWMA - indicating that the balance between buyers and sellers has tipped - you have exhausted the short term profit potential of the trade.

It's worth keeping an eye on the news pages by the way. If a breakout happens along with fundamental news, such as a positive earnings surprise or a new product launch, it's probably a real breakout - and some serious institutional funds may back it.

Plus - don't give up! This could be part of the consolidation, the build-up - the last unsuccessful test of resistance before the *real* breakout. Patience is well rewarded.

Stop-losses

Set your stop-losses tight for breakouts. If a breakout reverses, it could be fast and hard. The ideal for a breakout, though, is that if you've read the signals right, it should make money from the moment you enter the trade.

So most traders put a stop-loss just below the resistance line. If the price falls back here, it could fall away pretty sharply back into the old trading range, so stop yourself out of the trade. But remember that stocks will often retest the level they have just broken within the first few days, and then rise again - so don't set your stop-loss at or above the resistance line, just a bit below. Only take your loss if the stock closes the day below the line.

Chapter 3 Quiz

1. What's a stop-loss?
    a) The price at which you will exit the trade if it goes wrong,
    b) An insurance policy,
    c) A kind of option.

2. What is a gap?
    a) A clothing store,
    b) When the stock opens much higher or lower than yesterday's closing price,
    c) The difference between the bid and ask price for a stock.

3. What indicator can help you tell the difference between real and false breakouts?
    a) Volume
    b) Moving average
    c) 52-week high-low

4. Define a break-out.
    a) A stock price breaks out of a trend channel or other pattern within which it has been trading,
    b) The Great Escape,
    c) The same as a gap.

5. Which of these is not a way of shorting a stock or index?
    a) A call option
    b) An inverse ETF
    c) Selling short on margin.

A.Z Penn

4

Chapter 4: The Four Types of Indicators You Need to Know

This is the chapter that's full of all the jargon you've been dreading. RSI, stochastics, MACD, oscillators, Bollinger bands - it's all here. This is a tough chapter to get through, and it's also going to be a long one, but two things will make your life easier.

First, you can divide all these indicators into four main families; an indicator will show you:
1. Trend,
2. Momentum,
3. Volatility, or
4. Volume.

A lot of them are just refinements of another indicator in the family. For example, once you understand what a trend indicator is for, it's easy to understand another trend indicator and what in particular you might use it for. It's like looking at a toolbox full of different tools - when you realize that all of them are either spanners, chisels, screwdrivers or drill bits, and they just happen to come in slightly different sizes and shapes, but each type of tool is used for the same kind of job, then life gets considerably easier.

Secondly, once you start trading, you'll soon find that you are spotting more better trades using some indicators than others. That lets you concentrate on a smaller number of useful indicators. So although you might have, let's say, fifteen sizes of spanner, you know there's one that fits almost every job you need to do on your sports bike, and another that you need for the Shimano gears, and the rest get left in the box almost all the time.

I should give a special mention to oscillators here. Basically, to oscillate means to swing, and the idea of an oscillator is that it's an indicator which swings around a central zero line. It may be expressed as a percentage or go from -1 to +1, and it can be derived from all kinds of calculations, but oscillators are broadly speaking only interesting when they do one of two things: (1) go to extremes, or (2) cross over the central line. They take a bit of getting used to.

You'll also find that some indicators will actually deliver you trading ideas, but other indicators are useful mainly as confirmation, or as advance alerts. For instance, I'd never expect a volume indicator to give me a trading signal, but if the volume isn't there to support a breakout, I probably won't make the trade. So you won't be looking at all of these indicators all the time - just the ones that give you the signals, and once you've got a signal, then the other indicators come into play to tell you if it's real or fake.

And a little extra tip - if you open up a charting program while you're reading this chapter, get a stock chart up, and then call up each of the indicators (usually in drop-down boxes), you'll get a feel for how the indicators look "live".

I like using StockCharts. As you can see from the image below, you get lots of options, for instance, 'range' means you can select different date ranges, whether you want a month or ten years. You can define 'type', candlesticks if you want, or a single line, or OHLC, whichever you find gives you the best feel for the price movements.

Under 'Overlays', you can get moving averages and Bollinger bands, and a load of other more advanced stuff. You can have three moving averages or just two.

Then 'Indicators' has drop-down boxes letting you select plenty of indicators, including most of the ones we'll be talking about - RSI, MACD, Chaikin Money Flow, Force Index, and so on. So there's a lot of power in this platform for you to explore.

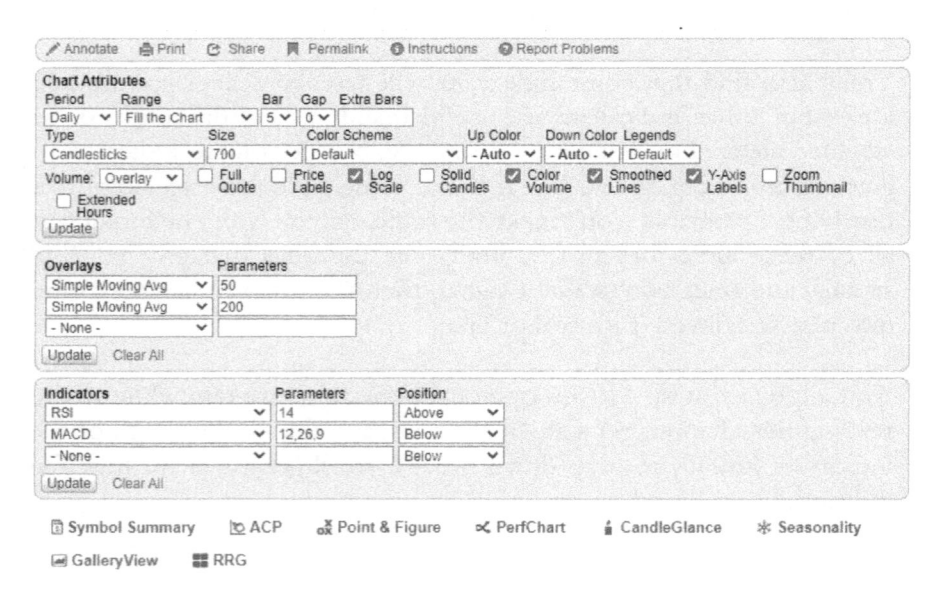

P.S. In Class 5 of the free bonus #1 companion masterclass, I demonstrate some practical ways of how you can use some of the indicators discussed in this chapter with real life chart examples. I would highly recommend you watch the free masterclass video after you finished reading this entire chapter by visiting: www.az-penn.com.

Trend indicators

You might well be able to look at a chart with the naked eye and spot the trends. But there's a lot of 'noise' in a stock price chart. Trend indicators use mathematical formulas to smooth out the noise and display the underlying trend in share prices in a way that makes it easier for you to pick up what's really going on.

Note that trend indicators always lag the trend, because they use past pricing data. For instance, a 20-day moving average uses the past 20 days' prices, so it will move more slowly than stock prices if they change direction. Trend indicators are trend *following* indicators, not trend *setting* indicators. That is, they won't tell you what's *going* to happen - they tell you a trend has already started, which can give you really strong trading signals. So they are not a faster way to get into a trade. They are best to trade in trending markets. In a sideways market, they're not all that useful, and if you try to trade a sideways market with them, you'll probably lose money.

Simple moving averages (SMAs)

A simple moving average just takes a number of time periods - say 10 days (which is two working weeks); it adds together the closing price for each day and divides by ten. So it's the average price of the stock over the last ten days. You can calculate it over any period - 20 days, 200 days, a year (though a year is probably not very useful for a trader). Or rather, you can get a chart package to calculate it for you, these days.

Why do we use simple moving averages? We use them to take the 'noise' out of the chart so that you can see the trend more easily. The idea is similar to trendlines, just a bit differently executed. But you should look at SMAs together with the price chart, because it's when you put the two together that you get the best information - and when you use two SMAs together, you can also get some interesting information.

For instance, when the price dips below a moving average, that's a sign that the stock might be breaking downwards. In this sense, an SMA can be treated a little like a resistance or support level. As a rule, in an uptrend, the price should be above the moving average - if it breaks down, this could be a strong signal that prices are shortly going to head downwards. But it's not got the best probability, so check with another indicator before you do anything about it.

The strategy of using crossing moving averages

Another way of using moving averages is to take two averages of different lengths, and to look for a significant crossover. All technical traders have their favorites; some like to use the 10 and 20 days MAs, others prefer 50 and 200 days, longer-term averages.

When the shorter-term MA crosses over the longer term, it gives you a bullish signal - the 'golden cross'. It's telling you that over the shorter period, on average, share prices have been trending higher than over the longer term. You might not see that so clearly from the actual price line, if the prices reported have been volatile. If the short term MA crosses to the downside, you have a 'death cross'. Prices are trending lower. That could be a good sell signal.

The problem, of course, is that while moving averages clarify what's happening, because the majority of a moving average is made up of older price data, they have a built-in time lag. And if a stock is trading in a range, in a fairly choppy way, you may find that the averages keep crossing over without delivering you any real information.

Look what happened here - this is a chart from Finviz, showing Graybug Vision. Look just at the end of February and you can see the purple 20-day average crosses the orange 50-day average, and keeps heading lower. At that point, Graybug was already down on its highs, but look how good a predictor that 'death cross' was in predicting the downtrend in the price.

Some traders use a three-MA system with a short, middle and long term MA, for instance, 5, 21, and 50 day averages. The trend is defined by whether the fast MA is above the middle MA (which shows an uptrend) or below the middle MA (which shows a downtrend). The signal is shown by the middle MA crossing the slower MA to the upside (that's a buy signal) or to the downside (that's a sell signal). You close your trade when the fast average crosses over the middle term average in the 'wrong' direction. I'm using the terms 'fast' 'middle' and 'slow' because for a day trader using 5 as the fast average, 21 might be his slow average, while for a medium term trader; 21 might be the fast average, and 200 the slow (using 21, 50, 200).

By the way, put some time into finding out which averages work best for you.

The three-average system can be confusing so let's just think about it with regard to a single buy trade. When the fast average is above the middle and slow averages, recent prices are rising. That might be just a temporary uptick. When the middle crosses the slow average to the upside, it shows that prices over the past month are now rising above prices further in the past, too.

That suggests a more continued trend. But if the fast average falls back below the middle average, it means the trend has decelerated, the last week has shown prices falling compared to the last month, so it's time to sell. (However, in *The Way of the Turtle*, Curtis Faith back-tested different strategies, and he found that while triple-MA trades have a higher win rate than dual-MA trades, they are not as profitable.)

As you can see from the chart below, you have a pretty messy and complex chart to read. Personally, I prefer the simplicity of just two MAs, but as they say, your mileage may differ. The zigzag line is the OHLC (Open-High-Low-Close) price line, and you then have a fast moving average in pink, a medium term moving average in yellow, and a slower moving average in light blue. You can see the fast MA sticks really close to the prices, while the slower MA is very sluggish and takes a long time to pick up. Notice that when the other two averages cross the slower MA right at the beginning of the chart, a strong uptrend starts, and you'd buy the stock here.

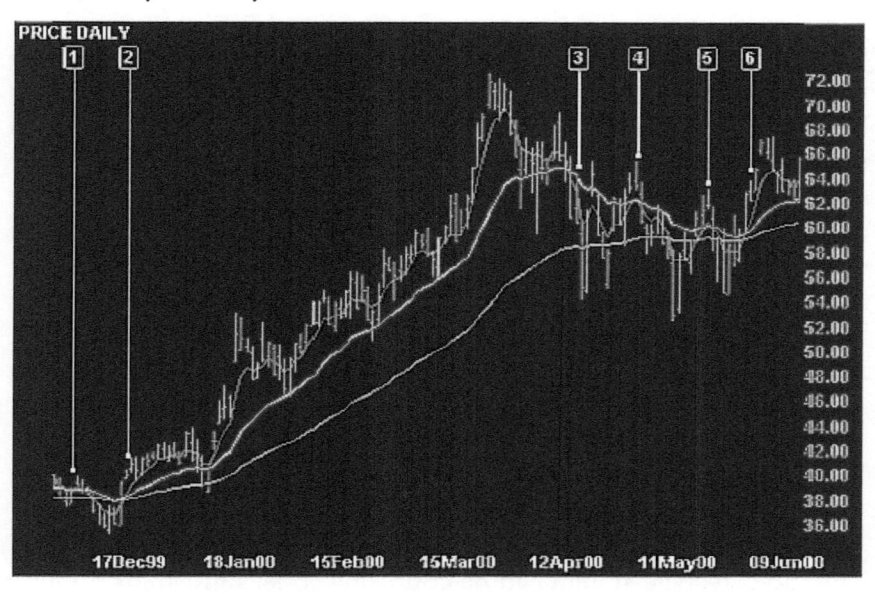

Now, if you hold on to the stock till the top, you'll see you wouldn't actually sell at the top. Instead, you'll lose some of your gains till the fast average falls below the medium one at point 3. But still, look how much you have made on the trade. From about $40 all the way to $54. That's a long term trade.

You could also take the 'swing' trades when those two moving averages cross over again; the trade at 4 doesn't work out at all, but it looks like the trade at 6 is a good one.

Remember, all your trades don't have to be winning trades. If you make 50/50 good trades, but you have tight stop-losses and let your profits run, you'll make money.

If you like to use MAs, you might play about with different lengths of time for your key MAs to see which work best for a stock or commodity you're interested in, or what's working best in the market at the moment. This does change from time to time as market conditions change and as other traders refine their technical analysis.

Exponential moving average (EMA)

The EMA takes the time lag problem and applies a bit of further mathematical manipulation to give the figures a recency bias, by giving more recent prices more weight. This makes them more timely, and many traders prefer them as the signals they give are likely to be slightly earlier than with the SMA. 12 and 26 day EMAs are particularly popular.

The EMA isn't 'shorter term' than the simple moving average, because all the same data is in there. The 12 day EMA still contains all 12 days. But it just gives a bit more weight to more recent ones.

In terms of all the kinds of signals you can find with EMAs, using them is exactly the same as using the SMAs. Why not try both to start with, if your charting package gives you a choice, and see whether it makes much difference which you use? It might be a good idea to 'backtest' - run both on charts for the past few years, and see how they compare in terms of how many trades you would have made with each, and how much you would have made in profit.

Moving Average Convergence/Divergence (MACD)

MACD develops the idea of a moving average a bit further still by adding even more math. It shows the difference between two different moving averages, whether they're getting closer together or further apart (the Convergence/Divergence in the name). And then we can get even smarter, and show a moving average of convergence and divergence.

Just so that you understand the calculation (you'll never have to do it, the software does it for you), we start off by taking a 12 and a 26 day EMA. When you eyeball the chart and look at those two moving averages, what you're doing is assessing the difference between them visually. MACD does this a different way by looking at it mathematically.

The MACD takes today's value of the 26-day EMA and subtracts it from the value of the 12-day EMA. That is today's difference between the two. Going forward, the same calculation gets done every day, and then you have a time series (a line of data) showing whether the difference between the two averages is getting smaller (convergence) or bigger (divergence).

So far, so good. But now to take the 'noise' out of the data, we make a moving average of the MACD. Typically, it's a 9 day EMA. That's then plotted on the chart and this is what we use as a 'Signal line'. And just to add some more visuals, the raw data of the Convergence and Divergence is often plotted as a histogram - a bar chart using the same space. Both the lines and the histogram use the same centerline, representing zero - both moving averages in sync with each other.

Okay, you don't necessarily understand why it works, but let's look at *how* it works.

The chart below shows what happened to Intel shares. I've blue-circled the two interesting indicators here. The MACD chart is at the bottom. First of all, the MACD heads up to the top of its range, having crossed the center line just about the beginning of 2021. So crossing the center line was the first alert, then moving up, about 22nd January. And then just before 16th February, the 50-day moving averages crosses over the 200 day in the price chart. That's the final signal that we have an uptrend. The MACD would suggest to buy at about $56 around 22nd January, and the stock runs as high as $63 before losing its momentum.

The MACD can give us a couple of useful signals. First, when the MACD line crosses the centerline. If it heads above it, buy; if it falls below it, sell. Secondly, when the MACD line crosses the Signal line (the average of the MACD, remember); if the MACD is headed up, buy, and if it heads down, sell. A rapid rise or fall in the MACD is also worth noting; it is likely to indicate that the stock is overbought or oversold, and that the current price trend will slacken off.

Although the histogram is not there to give you signals, it's a useful indicator for confirming other signals. When the blue bars are far below the line (in the negative numbers), prices are trending down; when the blue bars are above the line (in the positive numbers), the stock is in an uptrend. If you follow the 'humps' in the histogram, you also get a good sense for where the market could face a decision point - though you'll need to look at other indicators to see what that signal is. Here, for instance, you can see that the 'humps' are starting to build up from mid-November before the stock price makes its run up from 23rd November into early December. The histogram indicated the stock was already in an uptrend, though looking at the price chart you might not have got the idea.

Average Direction Index (ADX)

The ADX is an indicator some traders use to measure the strength of a trend. It was originally used in the commodity markets, though now it's used in other markets as well. I'm not going to go into how it's calculated; the formula is complex, with two different factors (sometimes also shown as separate lines) showing +DI and -DI - direction upwards and downwards, and these are then smoothed again to produce the ADX figure. Readings below 20 show that the trend is weak or non-existent; readings above 40 show a very strong trend.

If you spot an interesting possible breakout on the price chart, check out the ADX. Very often, a low ADX will give you confirmation that the existing trend is weak, and that gives a breakout a good chance of succeeding. But remember - the ADX says nothing about what direction the share price is headed!

Not every chart service gives you ADX. StockCharts does - here, it's the line above the price chart (the blue and red lines are moving averages). So let's see what the ADX tells us. A very weak trend at the beginning, and you can see from the chart that the price was just dodging about, going nowhere. Then a much higher ADX as the price went up after Nov 16th, but although the price kept going up, the ADX flattened out after 7th December. And then you have some sideways trading and the ADX flattens out again and tells you there's no strong trend; so if you spotted bear signals in any other indicators right then, the ADX would have told you to go along and take the trade. But the ADX *doesn't* see the bounce up in March coming, and right now in April it's looking weak even though (without looking too closely) some of those candlestick formations are suggesting we might have a bounce coming. So, you see, ADX can be useful, but don't rely on it. It's just sometimes, if you like, the tie-breaker when you can't decide whether to trade or not.

Force index

The Force index includes price *and* volume factors, so it doesn't just look at what price stock was traded at, but also at how much stock was traded. So if the shares go down $2, but only a few are traded, it shows a lower number than if the shares fall $2 on very heavy volume. The daily values are smoothed into an exponential moving average, usually over 13 days, and then it's shown as an oscillator - a line that moves above and below zero. When it heads above zero, it's showing an uptrend (higher prices, more volume), and below zero, it's showing a downtrend (lower prices, less volume).

Because it includes the volume of trading, as well as the price, it sometimes captures information you wouldn't get from a purely price-based indicator. For instance, if prices are still moving higher but the Force index is falling, then the volume must be dropping. That might suggest buying interest is fading out, and if this continues, it could eventually lead to the market topping out. But while the Force index is a useful confirmation for price signals, relatively few traders use this indicator to produce signals itself.

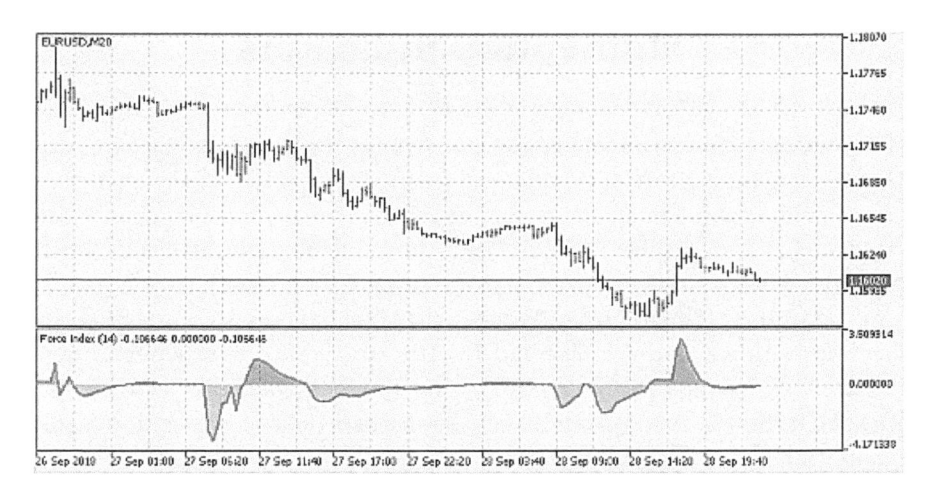

Here you can see the Force Index under the price chart. It's interesting how it shows the short term moves pretty well (first quarter of the chart) - look at the way it starts heading down at around 27 Sep 05:20, just before that big fall in price - but it has nothing at all to say about the longer term trend. And the second big blue peak doesn't give an advance warning of the rise in price; it happens at the same time. In fact, as a chartist, the big thing I see looking at that chart is a long term downtrend that I think is going to continue after what looks like a false breakout on 20 Sep 14:20, and the Force Index doesn't add anything to my knowledge. It's very much a short term indicator in my book, and this may be why many forex traders love it, but rather fewer equity traders seem to use it apart from a few day traders.

Momentum indicators

Momentum indicators aim to replace your eyeballing a price chart with something a bit more scientific and quantitative. They compare prices now with past prices, in order to show how strongly prices are trending. You could look at the momentum indicators as your speedometer - how fast is the stock going? The basic calculation is; momentum = (closing price today divided by closing price *x* days ago), and sometimes that's multiplied by 100, to deliver you a percentage figure. It's easy. And you're not going to do it, because let's face it, StockCharts' or Ameritrade's data banks can do it a whole lot faster than you.

But just as an illustration; last week the stock was at $50, and it's gone up to $75, momentum is 75/50 * 100 = 150% (or 1.5 for some indices). If the stock last week was $50 and now it's at $25, momentum is 25/50 * 100 = 50% or 0.5.

You may have guessed, if the stock price is flat, this index would give you 1, or 100%.

Momentum indicators won't usually give you signals, but they are useful as confirmation for your trading ideas. For instance, you can confirm a breakout if the momentum indicator has moved from the 98-99% range to 101% or 102% - the momentum has changed, that is, the stock's changed direction. If it keeps picking up further, that confirms your breakout will keep going. Use them to cut down the number of breakout trades that are stopped out when they turn out to be fake-outs, and you can increase your winning percentage considerably.

Momentum indicators are also interesting when they show *divergence*. If a stock price is still going up, but the momentum indicator is showing that it's putting the brakes on, that's a danger signal. It's like a train slowing down, which usually means there's a station coming up! If the share price is still headed lower, but the momentum indicator is coming back towards 100%, that shows the momentum behind the fall has started to fade away.

That's like a downhill skier slowing down as they come to the flat area at the bottom of the mountain. A breakout could be imminent - but that's where my analogy falls to pieces, because share prices don't get chairlifts...

When I started doing TA, I found these indicators were the most difficult to get my head around, even though my background included plenty of data manipulation and stats. I didn't find them as intuitive as, say, price charts or candlesticks. So if you have a tough time with some of them, you're not the only one.

Stochastic

The word 'stochastic', if you look it up in the dictionary, doesn't suggest this is a great indicator; 'stochastic' means "having a random probability distribution that can be analyzed statistically but not predicted precisely." And we're interested in predictions, so just how useful is a stochastic indicator going to be?

However, the stochastic is quite a good speedometer for stocks. Its inventor, George Lane, actually saw it in those terms - if a rocket is going to come down to earth and crash, it has to slow down at the top of its parabola. Planes only stall when they go too slowly.

How it works is by measuring the price range over a specific time period (typically 5 days). It compares the closing price each day with the absolute high and absolute low of the whole five days. So when it's at a high value, it means prices are closing towards the top of the range; a very low value means there's a high downside momentum. The Stochastic doesn't show 'oversold' or 'overbought', though - it simply shows the speed of price rises. As a comparison, imagine yourself going at 120 mph in your car - that's a high speed, but it doesn't mean you're immediately going to slow down. You might keep going for quite a while.

It *is* a really good confirmation for breakout signals from the price chart. If the stochastic keeps moving up steeply, it suggests the trend will continue - so if you bought on a price signal for a breakout, and the price has gone up, you should keep your trade running, perhaps scale in, and pull your stop-losses up to take account of the new entry price.

Another kind of signal is given when the price has been going up and up, but the stochastic starts to trend downwards. Even if this is quite a small divergence, and the stochastic line is just sagging a little bit, then you might want to look for a reversal. The stochastic is telling you that things are slowing down - and while that might just mean the price rise becomes less steep, if the stock has had a lot of buying interest, and risen quite steeply, the stochastic could be warning you that things are going to get bumpy. If there's no buying pressure left, the stock might fall quite fast.

The same signal works the other way around if prices have been coming down, but you see the Stochastic lift up - reversal could be on the cards. This is probably the one time that the Stochastic gives a good signal rather than just a confirmation.

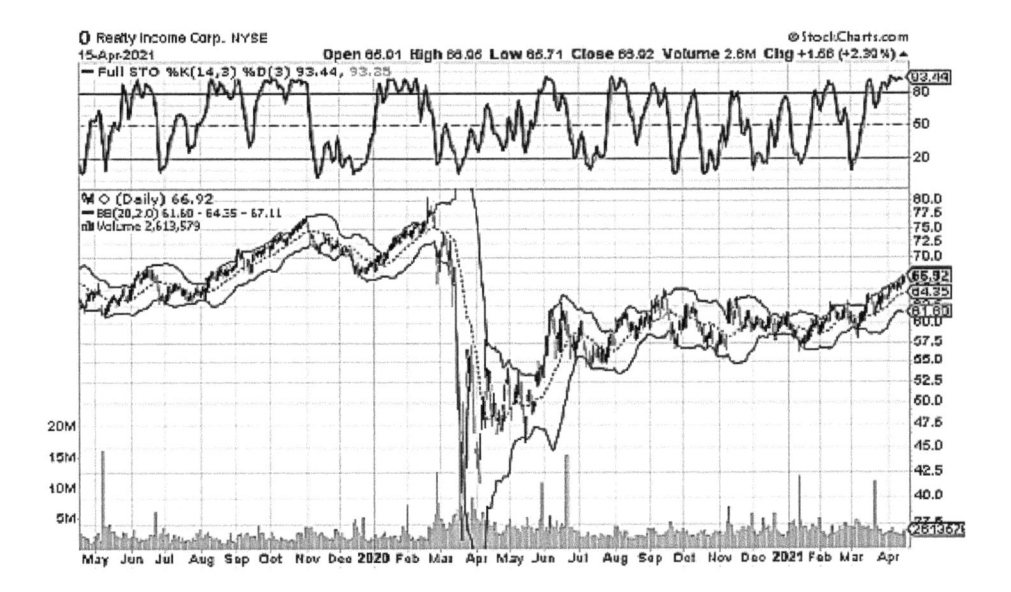

This chart shows the full stochastic at the top. Realty Income is one of the most well-regarded US real estate stocks and pays big dividends. Look how much the stochastic swings. Interestingly, the big moves into negative territory often come before a downturn, and the big swings upwards just before an uptrend. (Of course, you have to remember that the huge downturn in March was event-driven; this was the start of the Covid-19 pandemic in the west. I don't think the stochastic is really predicting that! But if you'd taken notice, you would be a bit richer, anyway.)

Relative Strength Index (RSI)

This index measures the ratio of upwards to downwards price moves. It doesn't look at how big the rise or fall was, but simply whether the stock closed up or down on the day. So, for instance, a 10-day RSI starts by looking at how many days was the stock up? 7. And down? 3. (If the stock closes level on the day, it gets a zero for that day.) Then the figures are averaged, so we get plus 7/10 and minus 3/10. (That's a simple way to do it. Other people use EMA and advanced statistical smoothing methods, which are only going to confuse you, so let's leave that out.)

And now all we have to do is calculate the ratio between the up and down moves, RS, and then the RSI = 100 − (100 / (1 + RS)).

If you've followed that, then you have probably guessed that the index goes from 0 to 100. If you haven't followed it, it doesn't matter. You've got the idea, anyway; the RSI is a measure of how often the price is rising, against how often it's falling. Usually, stocks will trade somewhere between 30 and 70 on the RSI, and that shows a reasonable balance of buyers and sellers. But an RSI above 70 shows that the stock is probably overbought - so the price could be about to fall - whereas if the index is below 30, the stock is oversold, so the price might be about to rise. (Some traders prefer to use an 80-20 range for their trades, which gives them fewer but higher probability signals.)

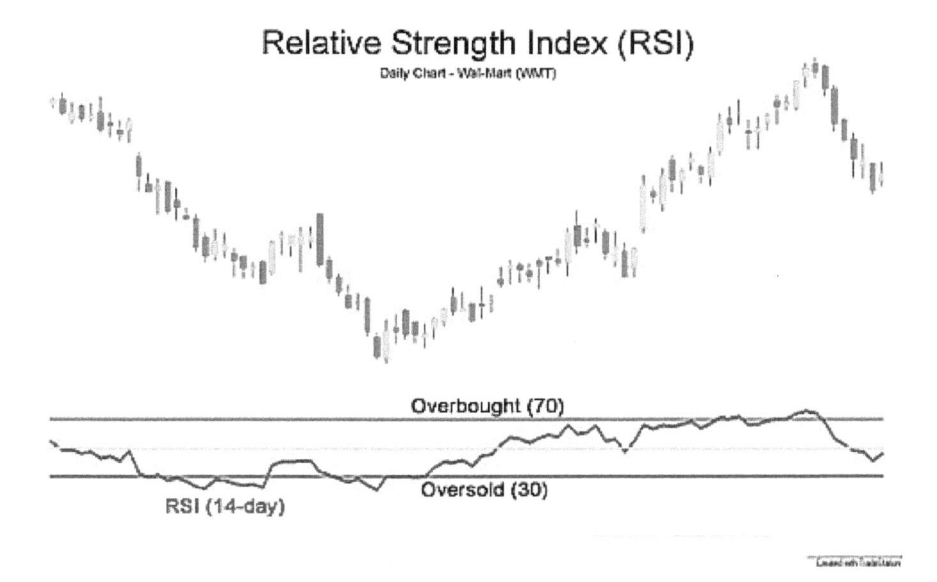

Relative Strength Index (RSI)
Daily Chart - Wal-Mart (WMT)

In the chart above, you can see how when the RSI dips below the 30 line the first time, the price stages a small rally, but the second time it's for real - too many sellers have been in the second stage of the downtrend and when there's a breakout, it really moves fast. Then when the RSI gets close to 70, there's a small dip, but it isn't till it crosses over the 70 line that the price really tanks. By then, just too many people have bought in, some have bought too much stock, and the moment the price decline begins, they 'catch a cold' and sell. You might like to think about the RSI line having just crossed over the center line (the straight line in light blue); will it stay around that level? Could it be heading for oversold territory?

What do we mean by 'overbought' and 'oversold'? When a stock is overbought, it may have had lots written about it in the press, many investors have been buying, the price has kept moving up, but now, everyone who wants the stock has got some. There are no newer buyers to push the price up. And a few of the early buyers might want to take a profit, which would be a catalyst for a downwards price move. With 'oversold', the stock has seen many sellers who want out, maybe because of poor earnings performance or a dividend cut, and now everyone who wanted to sell has sold. If a few contrarian buyers enter the market thinking the stock looks cheap, it could rise.

RSI is particularly good at picking up the bottom of a long fall or the top of a spike, where the price chart might not be telling you anything useful at all. If you want to get in towards the bottom of a market correction, watch the RSI! If you want to avoid being stuck with too much money in the market at the very top of a bull market, watch the RSI!

Most traders use the 14-day RSI. Depending on the time periods you prefer to trade, you might pick 9 (for day traders) or 30 (for medium term traders).

There are several ways to use RSI. First, it gives you a good feel for trends. If the RSI breaks its trendline, this might be the first indication that a reversal could be on the cards *before* seeing it in the price chart.

Secondly, you should look for RSI divergence. Look to see when the RSI is doing the opposite of the price line. When a price makes a higher high, look for the previous highest high, and draw a line connecting the two. Now look at the RSI underneath on your price chart, and do exactly the same - look for the most recent highest high, which may not be exactly underneath the share price's high, and draw a line connecting it to the previous highest high. Now look at the direction of the two lines. If they're going in the same direction, that's great. That's the way you'd expect it to be - the price is going up, and the stock is closing most days up rather than down. But if the RSI line is headed downwards, and not up like the share price, it's a bad sign - you have what is called bearish *divergence* and that's a good sell signal.

Price Rate of Change (ROC or PROC)

This is another oscillator, an indicator that goes from 0 to 100 and back again. (Most of these oscillators are 0-100, but they could be expressed as 0 to 1 as well - we just use 100 because it's easier to read than having decimal points all over the place. 77 is easier than 0.77 and it uses less ink. Or fewer pixels.) Think of price charts as a map; oscillators are speedometers.

It shows the rate of change in the price over a period, with a bit of smoothing - unlike the stochastic which measures the price compared with the price *range*.

ROC is centered on a line representing zero, so it shows how much prices are increasing (above the line) or falling (below the line). Usually, it's calculated on a 9-day basis; 14 and 25 are also used. There's probably a good reason for this, but it seems to be lost in the mists of time. When you're looking at a particular stock or market, find out which is the best for your needs. A very volatile stock might be better analyzed using one of the longer ROC periods, like 25 days.

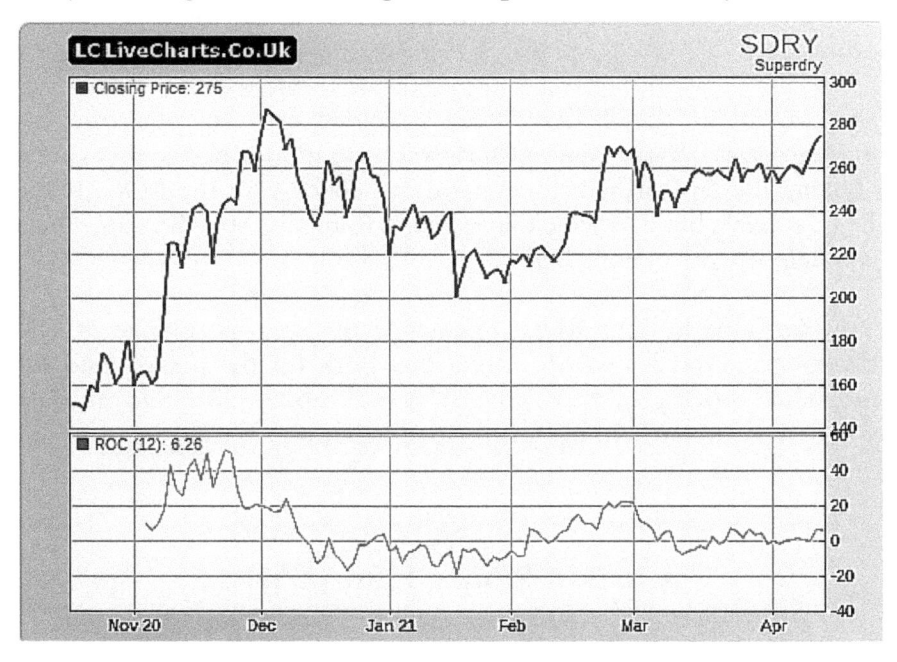

This chart is for UK stock Superdry and comes from LiveCharts. I've deliberately taken out all the information except for the ROC at the bottom and the price line. You can see how the ROC shoots up at the start of the chart in mid-November, but then falls towards the centerline zero in mid-December.

If you sold when the ROC had got to 20 in early December, you'd have sold pretty close to the peak of just over 280p - if you waited till ROC crossed the center line in mid-December, you'd still have got out at 240p before it the price fell back to 200p in mid-January. Later on, the next move up happens just as the ROC line crosses zero again, at the beginning of February.

ROC is a nice timing tool to use within trends and to confirm trading ideas. Some short term traders like to trade when the ROC crosses the centerline. But for this to work, you should either have your moving averages in a bullish formation (i.e., the short term above the longer term average), or you should see the averages moving towards a golden cross.

Or you might already have seen a golden cross in your moving averages, towards the bottom of the recent trading range so that you're "buying the dip", in which case you can check with the ROC. If the ROC is weak, but it's rising, that suggests things are speeding up, which will help the price move higher.

You can also look at ROC divergence the way we looked at RSI divergence. And it's worth noting that both for the market and for individual stocks, an ROC that stays well above 50 could indicate you're moving into bubble territory, so it can be a warning sign.

Chaikin Money Flow (CMF)

This oscillator aims to measure buying pressure, or accumulation, against selling pressure or distribution. Chaikin oscillates between +100 and -100 (or +1 and -1). Chaikin differs from ROC or RSI because it builds trading volume into the equation as well as price and gives more weight to price movements that occur on strong trading volume.

With some charting programs, the zero line Chaikin shows as red, above as green. A stock that you're looking to break out or continue upwards is more likely to do so if the Chaikin band is mainly green; if there's a lot of red in the Chaikin band, you might want to reconsider that trade or cut your initial position and set a tight stop-loss. On the other hand, if you see lots of red in the Chaikin oscillator, and you fancy shorting a stock - that red is a good sign!

But even if you don't get the traffic light signals, Chaikin usually gives a strong visual signal as you'll see a really big hump of bars if it is strong.

Chaikin divergence can sometimes give you a good idea of a stock that's looking exposed. If a stock price rallies, but the Chaikin indicator is still in the red, that means the rally is based on very little volume. A pullback is much more likely when that is the case. On the other hand, if the Chaikin oscillator is nice and green, it's likely that the rally will continue.

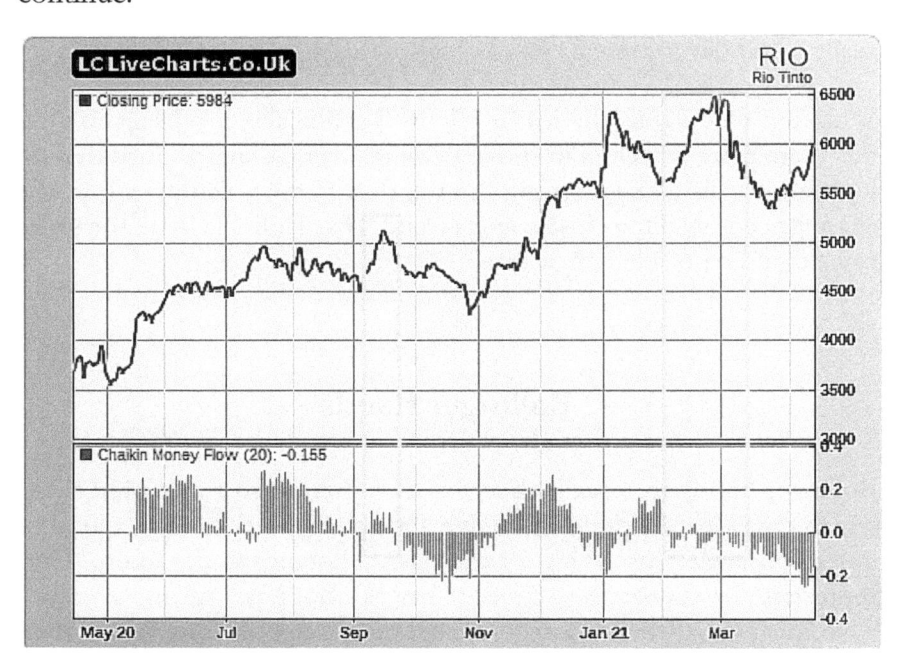

Another UK stock - this is global miner RTZ. If you look at the rallies that I've marked in yellow, the Chaikin Money Flow tells me that they're not really supported by much money. So I'd expect them to fade out, and they do. On the other hand, the rise between November and January is, at least at first, quite well supported by the CMF, so if there's a golden cross in the moving averages too, it may be worth going along for the ride.

Volatility indicators

Volatility indicators have a different focus from momentum indicators. They don't tell you how fast prices are moving, but how jerkily - whether the share price is making smooth progress, or whether it's all over the place. High volatility shares tend to be ones where no one is really sure what the price ought to be - they might shoot up from $100 to $115 one day, and fall to $90 the next - whereas a low volatility share might trade around $100 all the time, sometimes as low as $97 if it's really a bad day, or maybe just as high as $104.5.

What does a volatility indicator tell us? Technically, it tells us how far the share price is willing to move from its average trend. Turn that on its head; it tells us how strong the trend is. If the volatility is low, the share price is sticking closely to its trend. If volatility is high, the share price could be headed anywhere.

Bollinger Bands

Bollinger Bands are usually shown as two thin lines or a colored cloud which envelops the price chart. I've always regarded them as a kind of 'price sausage'. They work on the basis of standard deviation. They represent the *distribution* of recent prices about the mean (average). That means that they adjust to changes in price volatility. Remember, if the price is jumping around a lot, it has a high standard deviation, and if it's pretty flat or in a stable trend, it has a low standard deviation.

The top band is one standard deviation *above* the moving average, and the bottom band is one standard deviation *below*. Since the share price is usually (though not always) somewhere inside, that gives you your 'sausage'!

Finding it hard to visualize? Okay, here's an example from Bigcharts. It's Proctor & Gamble over the last year. Take a look where there's a squeeze in the sausage, so to speak. July - a big squeeze followed by an uptrend. Mid-September, another squeeze followed by a small uptrend. Then the share price goes nowhere till the next squeeze at the beginning of 2021, and suddenly there's a new downtrend. Interesting, hm?

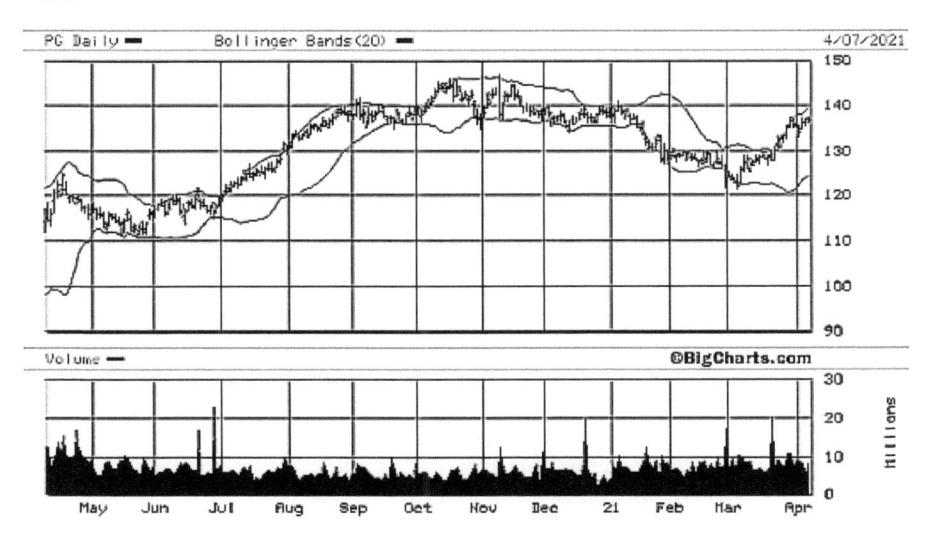

Bollinger Bands will not give you a signal. But they can help you assess whether a price signal is a good one or not. For instance:

- "The squeeze" - When volatility is low and the bands tighten even more, a sharp price movement becomes more likely. But that move could be in either direction, and there could be a false move in the wrong direction first.
- When the bands get really far apart, volatility is high and existing trends may break down.

- If prices are generally sticking to the top band, a stock may be overbought and there could be a downwards move in prospect. On the other hand, if prices are glued to the bottom band, and you spot a breakout on another indicator, the stock's likely to be oversold which means there could be a quick lift-off.
- Prices sometimes have a habit of bouncing within the bands, so if in a chart where a stock's behaving that way I see a bounce off the bottom band, I'll probably check out the top Bollinger Band as a potential medium term price target, and maybe the moving average as a shorter term target.

Worth knowing: Bollinger Bands have nothing to do with Bollinger champagne - except that if you learn to read them well, you'll be able to afford a few bottles of bubbly.

Average True Range (ATR)

The ATR shows you in a single line how volatility changes over time. Unlike previous indicators which generally take the closing price, ATR was designed for markets like commodities which frequently gap up or down, or make limit moves (that is, the exchange stops them trading if the price moves more than a certain amount). So ATR looks at the true range of price as being the greatest of these three comparisons:
1. the current high less the current low, or
2. the current high less the previous close, or
3. the current low less the previous close.

All these numbers are used as positive values (even if the biggest variation was downwards, it's not shown as a negative number). The average over a number of periods (usually 14) is then calculated.

Because it's shown as an absolute figure, you can't compare ATR between stocks. Google (Alphabet) shares are worth $2020 and can go up or down more than $50 a day; Cisco shares are worth $50 and don't usually move more than $1.5.

And because it's an absolute number, it shows *only* price volatility - high values could reflect prices are dropping or soaring; all you know from the ATR is that the movement was extreme.

If you see what looks like the beginning of an uptrend, check the ATR. If the ATR is increasing, that uptrend is getting some support. But if the ATR hasn't moved much, the impetus or 'push' behind the uptrend may fade away - this might help you decide not to make the trade.

Wow, look at that. Right at the start of the chart, Cisco started an uptrend in early November, and you can see the ATR shoot right up. It's really got some oomph. And then the ATR falls away in late November, even though the price chart is still in an uptrend for a while.

You wouldn't want to short it at the $43-45 price level where the ATR starts really falling away, but if you look at the return you'd get for holding on to the shares during December-January, and then think you could have had your money in a much more interesting situation like a massive breakout... as a trader you would want to be out of there and into the other stock, or waiting around two months until February for a bit more action in Cisco...

Volume indicators

Here's our last set of indicators. The previous indicators have all told us about the way the share price is behaving. Volume indicators, on the other hand, tell us nothing about price. They tell us how much stock is being traded.

You might think, "The price is going up! Why do I need to know how much stock is changing hands? That's nothing to do with the price!" But I can tell from my own experience, as well as many other experienced (and profitable) traders, that volume is one of the most important indicators of all. It's the lie detector of price trends. It's the fake-finder. It's the fraud-buster.

If an apparent price trend isn't accompanied by an increase in volume, it might be fake. If it is accompanied by very thin volume, it's definitely a fake. Learn to check the volume indicator just like you check your rearview mirror before turning left. It's a life-saver!

Intraday volume

If we look at the volume traded during the average day, it's not evenly distributed. From half to three-quarters of stock is traded during either the first or the last hour of the trading day - the open or the close. No one trades much at lunchtime.

At the open, traders are reacting to yesterday's close and this morning's news, or perhaps fundamental analysts have made calls in the morning meeting on a stock that announced earnings yesterday that are the reverse of the initial market sentiment. All this gets done first thing.

Then in the last hour, you've got traders squaring their positions, closing positions they don't want to hold overnight, and investors reacting to news that came through today.

That means if you're a day trader and you're trying to follow volume, you never really know what the volume for the day is going to be till the close. There could be high trade in the morning and then nothing all day.

You can have a good guess though. You know the average daily volume traded per stock. So you can split that up, about 40% in the first hour, 40% in the last hour, the rest spread (or perhaps a third in the first hour, to be conservative.) Then, if at the end of the first hour, a stock has traded 52% of its average daily income, you know it's well ahead of where it ought to be at this time of day.

Let's do a little charting. Go to Bigcharts or StockCharts, and I want you to get a five-day chart of IBM, showing the price hourly, and showing the volume. Can you see how the volume spikes up at the beginning and end of each day? Try it with Cisco or Microsoft. It should be about the same. The only time it's different is when you get a big announcement or news in the middle of the day.

Unless you're a day trader, other volume indicators are less work and will be more suited to your trading style than this one, though.

Volume by Price

Volume by price shows the amount of volume for a given price range. The calculation is based on every trade in a given period, at a given frequency, so you could have
- A six-month chart of daily closing prices,
- A two-week chart of price and volume every half-hour
- A five-year chart of price and volume each week.

You'll see the Volume by Price displayed as a bar chart with horizontal bars to one side of your price chart. Here's one from TrendSpider, a paid-for software that gives you alerts, scanning and the ability to backtest your trading rules as well as charting software. Here, the Volume by Price is shown by grey bars on the right hand side. What's the interest in knowing volume by price? It shows you how much volume has been traded *at a given price level*. That often turns out to be a support or resistance zone for the share price. Here, you can see that there are two particularly large bars that correspond to a support/resistance level.

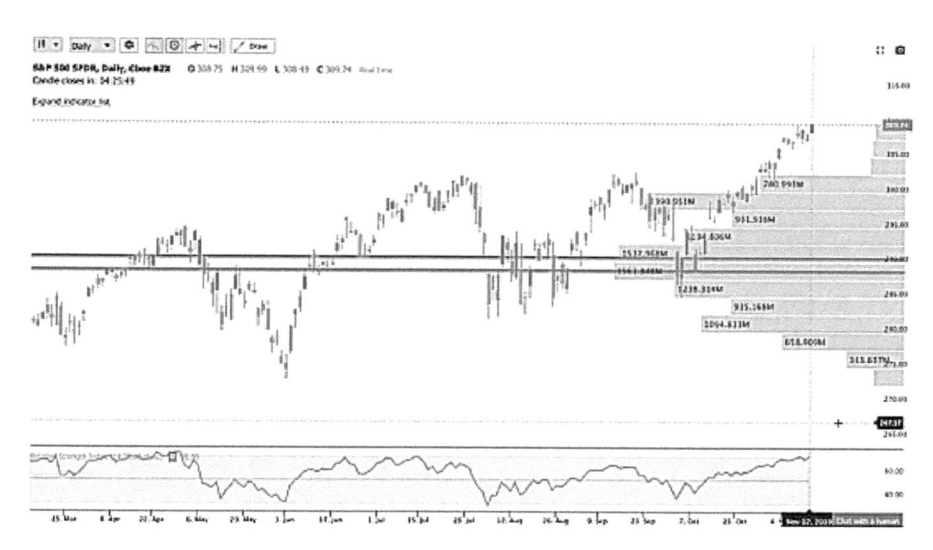

And some charting software goes further - it colors the horizontal bars for Volume by Price in green or red. It assumes that if the price ended the day down, it was driven by selling, and contrariwise if the stock price went up, the bulls were in charge of the markets. So the longest bars show areas where there has been the most demand to buy (more green in the bar) or sell (more red in the bar) the stock over the period for which you ran the chart.

Obviously, for every seller, there's a buyer. But in any given market, you get a feeling for who's in charge. You may find it easier to understand thinking about real estate - when it's a 'buyer's market' prices are going up, everyone wants to buy real estate, if you put your house on the market, you might get competing buyers bidding each other up; when it's a 'seller's market' you'll be lucky to get people viewing and they'll probably ask for a better price, a new bathroom, or whatever. One side or the other is 'driving' the deals and that's what the green and red bars will tell you.

Accumulation/Distribution indicator (A/D)

This indicator shows the relationship between volume and price to determine the trend of a stock; the relation between price and demand may show accumulation (i.e., buying of stock) or distribution (i.e., more sellers). Basically, it's an application of the law of supply and demand by manipulating figures that we can easily get from the stock market. It's a cumulative value, adding the previous measure to todays to get the current value.

The A/D indicator is useful
- As a confirmation of trends, when it follows the share price closely;
- When it diverges from the price trend, and it suggests the price trend could change.

Be warned though that the A/D can peak or trough a month or two before prices do. So though you know prices are exposed, it's not a great indicator to trade on - it simply tells you that you should be looking for another signal, but when you do, it'll be a good one.

Using A/D together with the RSI is useful. RSI will show if the stock is likely oversold/overbought, and that may back up what the A/D indicator is telling you.

Take a look at March 8; Tesla shares hit a low, the A/D hits a low, the RSI just goes below 30 all at the same time here. So that says, hey, there's *gonna* be a bounce - and there is. And while the immediate bounce fades away a bit after hitting the 650-700 resistance level during mid-March, it does look as if an uptrend is beginning to establish with a series of steps up at the end of March. The A/D is a bit high right now but the RSI hasn't gone past 70 - if it did, I would definitely want to close out the trade, though.

On-Balance Volume (OBV)

OBV is a similar indicator with a slightly different approach. Instead of adding all the figures, it *subtracts* "down days" and *adds* days when the stock "closes up". What it's trying to do is to work out how much of the volume was driven by sellers, and how much by buyers.

The actual number isn't relevant - it depends on where you started. What's important is the trend, and the theory behind OBV. It's pretty interesting. OBV aims to pick up the difference between the big, institutional investors - professional fund managers, insurance companies, pension funds, and the like - and retail investors (whether that's the Robinhood crowd, buy-and-hold guys, or the kind of people who are stupid enough to take tips from taxi drivers).

When the price moves on slim volume, it may be driven by the Robinhood traders or a few retail investors taking a tip from CNBC. But when the price moves on big volume, it's going to be the big investors who are moving it. Ultimately they are the ones who move the market, so if you track what they're doing with the OBV indicator, you have the best chance of spotting the *real* price trend - what the smart money is doing.

That's the theory. Okay, we can all think of a stock where the mighty Wall Street hedge funds and the little retail traders had different views, right? GameStop - Redditors were buying like crazy and the hedge funds were going short. OBV doesn't really seem to do anything here. I really thought OBV would show all that big buying and selling peak to be on slim volume, but it doesn't. And I'm not really sure who was the 'smart' money here either, because if you were a retail trader who bought GME in November and sold any time since the beginning of 2021, you made a packet.

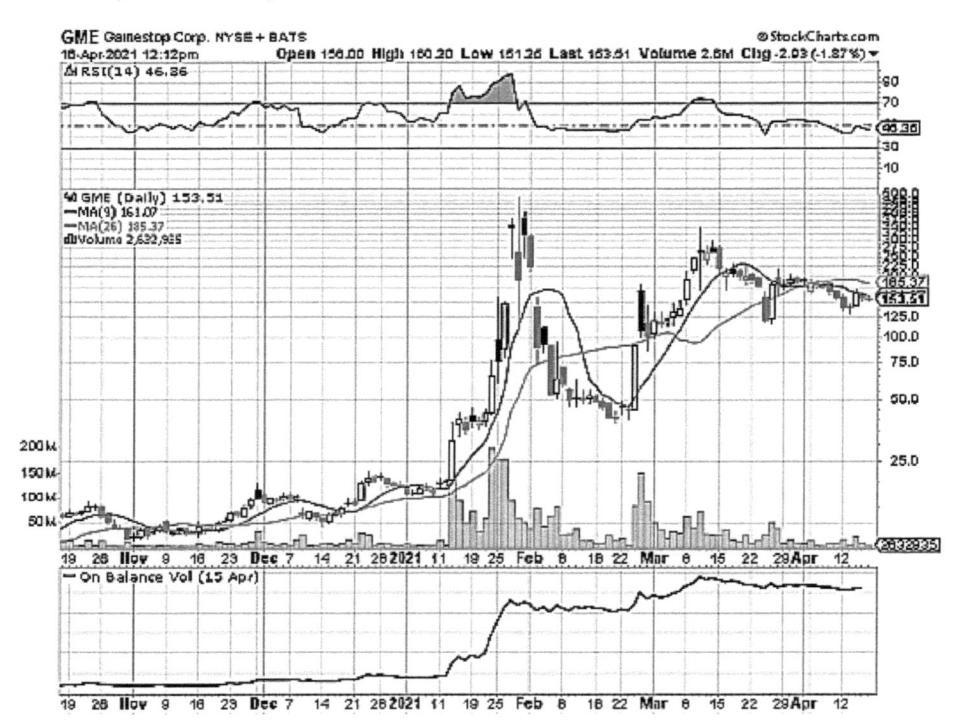

So you can see I'm not the biggest believer in this one - but it may work for you. You'll only find out by tracking it, along with all the other indicators, till you find out which one catches your eye most often and turns out to be giving you good information. I like moving averages and RSI best, and a friend of mine loves to have 3 or 4 oscillators open. He makes different trades, too, but we both make money. Watch out for spikes by the way. OBV can get thrown off course by the reaction to earnings or new product announcements.

A note before we go on

Okay, that's it for indicators. I bet you're feeling relieved! You may also be feeling a bit overwhelmed, and maybe some of those names and abbreviations are swimming around in your brain and getting mixed up. I packed into this chapter what takes many technical traders a good while to acquire. When I started out, I was using price and moving averages for a long time before I even discovered MACD.

So don't worry if you found this hard going. You can go on with chapter 5, which looks at patterns, so it's quite different - more visual, less mathematical and analytic - and come back to this chapter later. Or just stop reading for a while, let your whirling ideas settle down, and come back and read this chapter again.

Chapter 4 Quiz

1. Why are volume indicators so important?
    a) They tell you whether there is real money behind a move in the share price.
    b) They tell you whether you'll be able to sell your stock.
    c) They are just nice to know.

2. Why would you not go short if the A/D tells you we're at the top of the market?
    a) Going short is risky
    b) The A/D is often a month or so ahead of the trend
    c) The A/D is only a confirmatory indicator and doesn't give signals

3. What is RSI divergence?
    a. When the RSI changes direction
    b. When the RSI is trending in the opposite direction to prices
    c. When the RSI trades below 20

4. When the share price dips below a moving average, it's
    a) A potential bearish signal
    b) Just noise
    c) A sign of a breakout

5. Why is the ADX useful?
    a) It tells you the price trend doesn't have much impetus left in it,
    b) It tells you the price is going up,
    c) It tells you the price is going down.

A.Z Penn

5

Chapter 5: Continuation Patterns

Some types of patterns crop up again and again on price charts - like the cup and handle, triangles, and pennants. If you learn to recognize them, they can give a feel for what's likely to happen next. (I like to compare them to that creepy music in horror movies; it *might* just be there to get you on edge and Mom's going to come in with a cake, but then on the other hand, we know that *more often than not* it's the guy with the ax, the chainsaw or the knife.)

A continuation pattern suggests a price will continue in the same trend. It's a useful pattern to know. When you see a continuation pattern and it is completed successfully, the chances are good that the price will now continue in the same direction. But you do need to wait for the pattern to be completed, as some end in failure and trend reversal. Typically, you'll see the pattern building up, you'll see the completion and breakout, and you can then trade that breakout to catch the trend.

Continuation patterns are always most reliable when you see them within a strong trend - a small surfboard and big waves. If the share price is hardly trending either up or down, I wouldn't even bother looking for a continuation pattern. And a lot of them are prone to false breakouts, so remember to check for confirmation from other indicators.

Cup and handle

Cup and handle patterns are continuation patterns that you'll generally find in an uptrend - the 'cup' is a dip in the trend. The cup and handle pattern is difficult to describe and can be hard to spot, but you'll know it when you see it. (I think it looks more like a soup ladle, to be honest.) The first part is the 'cup', which is a price decline followed by an almost equal rise - if you draw a trendline freehand, you'll probably get some kind of parabola or U-shape. The next part is the 'handle', a triangle or sideways channel that should, as with normal cups, be smaller than the cup, and ideally remaining in the upper half or (even better) upper third of the cup. Look for a deep cup and a relatively shallow handle. But note that the handle can be pointing down, when you're expecting an uptrend to resume. That doesn't matter! The breakout will still be upwards.

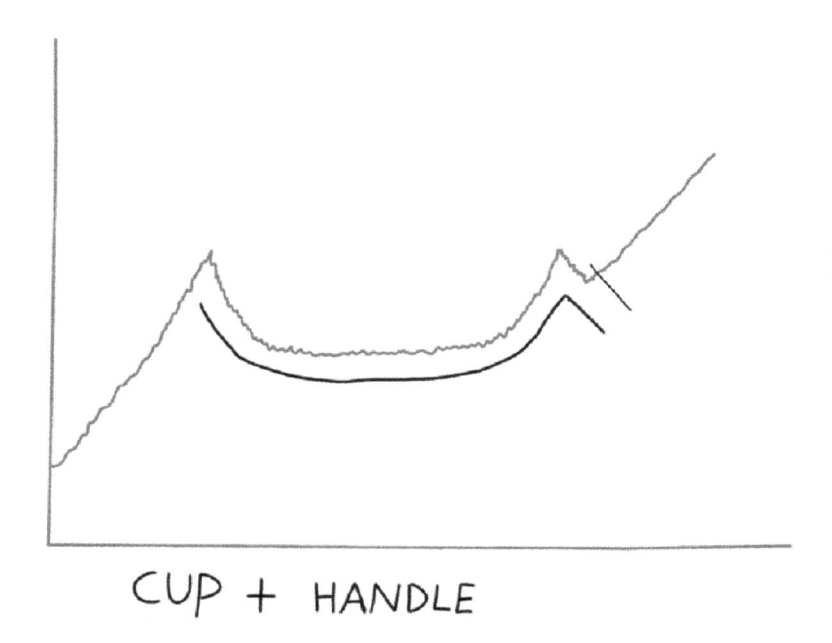

CUP + HANDLE

Never start trading with the 'cup'. The cup is just an alert that something is getting set up. It's the handle that tells you what's really going on. Let the handle get well established, and look for a breakout. When the breakout happens, it's time to trade. Most of the time, the cup-and-handle is a continuation pattern - it makes a pause in the trend, but then the share price rejoins the trend.

You're most likely to lose money on a failed breakout. Set your stop-loss at the bottom level of the handle, or at the most recent swing low within the handle. That means if, unusually, you've got a reversal, or if the breakout fails, you're covered. Meanwhile, your profit target is the breakout point, plus the total height of the cup. So if the cup is $30-35, and the breakout is $35, your target is $40. Your stop-loss will probably be around $33, so you have a 5:2 expected profit:loss ratio. That's not too bad.

Here's a real example, a cup and handle formation in McDonald's. On the left hand side of the chart you can see an uptrend, and looking at those candlesticks you'll also note it's almost entirely green - very few days closed down during the trend. Then it broke, almost exactly halfway through the chart at the beginning of November, and then after falling significantly it settled into a consolidation pattern forming the 'cup'. It hasn't really formed a handle yet, but that's potentially a nice deep cup if the pattern continues to work out.

Dead Cat Bounce

(I really hope you're a dog-lover!) A dead cat bounce (DCB) is a temporary uptick in a steady downtrend. The price goes up temporarily before the downtrend reasserts itself - a 'bounce', but not a reversal. Often, it's caused by bargain seekers thinking a stock must have reached the trough. Sometimes, traders who have been bearish simply want to cover their shorts and lock in some profit. So the price ticks up - but not for long.

Now here's the problem: how can we tell the real bottom from a DCB? You can't. This is why I don't advise you to short a DCB - if it turns out to be a breakout, you could lose a lot of money very, very fast.

On the long side, if you buy into a DCB, you risk seeing the stock price fall away sharply. (Of course, you should set a stop-loss which will stop you from being suckered into staying in the stock all the way down.) But if you *don't* buy into it real low, you'll miss the uptrend!

You can't tell the difference easily. So if you spot the DCB early, you can 'scalp' it - take a quick profit from the uptick and sell before the downturn resumes. A quick trigger finger and tight stop-loss controls are needed for this trade. A DCB can easily double the stock price before turning down again, so you might want to take partial profits on the upside - lock in a profit in case the stock turns down fast.

Your best bet is to build up your experience by paper trading till you have some gut feel for this play, and remember your trading rules. And remember, this is a short term play, and one which takes fast reactions. If you're more of a mid-term speculator, leave DCBs alone.

Triangle

This is a really common pattern to find, though it takes a little expertise to interpret correctly. The price trend starts to show convergence with lower highs, and higher lows - so that if you draw a line connecting all the highs, and a line connecting all the lows, you get a triangle. You're going to want to have at least two connecting points and ideally three so you can see this really is a triangle and not a random pattern. The closer the two lines of the triangle get, the more likely it is that you'll get a breakout, with the price breaking out of the triangle quite forcefully. That's the trade you're looking for.

Sometimes a triangle will be symmetrical. But it can also be an *ascending triangle*, where the highs draw a horizontal (or more gently sloped) line but the lows are rising - or it can be a descending triangle, in which case you have a horizontal line of lows and the highs are coming down to meet it. It is a medium term pattern, taking some weeks and in some cases even a couple of months to form.

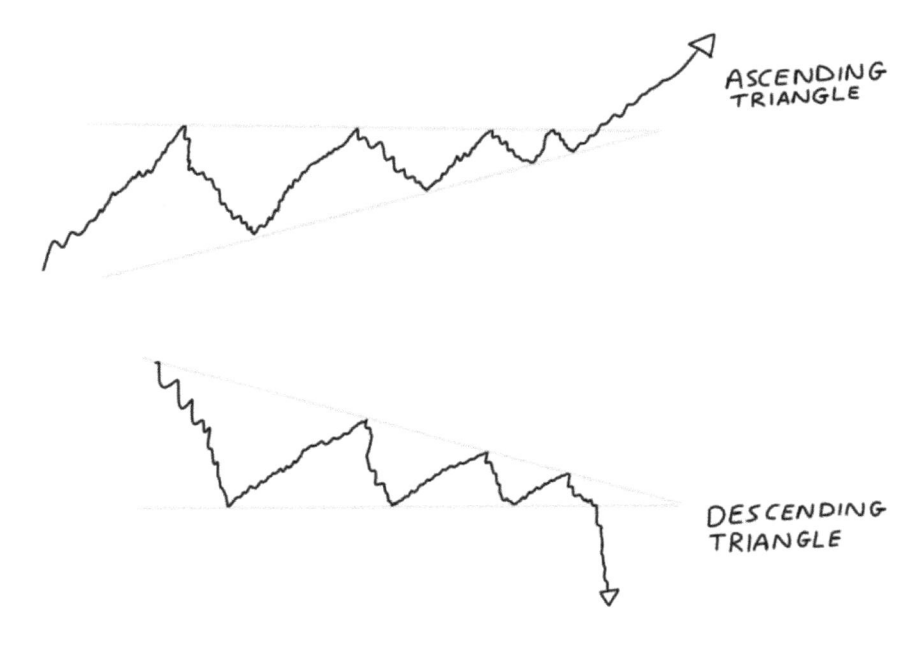

ASCENDING TRIANGLE

DESCENDING TRIANGLE

A *descending triangle* is a really strong pattern to trade. Remember, the price must already be in a downtrend. The triangle is just a consolidation within the trend. You're seeing lower and lower highs - buyers are unable to get the price going up. Meanwhile, the lows are providing a good solid support line. Once the price breaks below the support, you make your trade.

The chart above is one of the ones I found on Finviz when I asked it for descending triangles. The site automatically identifies patterns - they're not always 100% in my book, but sometimes they're real classics, and this I think could turn out to be a good trade… except that the price *wasn't* in a downtrend before the triangle got started.

The good thing about the triangle is that it tells you what profit to look for. Where the triangle started, measure the distance between the low and the highest price. That's your potential profit. Subtract that from the low, and you have your share price expectation for where you want to close the trade. So here as soon as the share price closed below the bottom line (and it hasn't yet), I'd want to go short, so a bit less than $15, and then looking at the difference between the blue line and that early December top, I'm looking for $1.50 profit - so a share price of $13.50 is my immediate target. Also, because it's not quite a classic pattern because of the uptrend, I'm going to look for some good volume backing the move downwards before I enter the trade. If the price bounces back just through the blue line, I'm not bothered, but I will set a stop-loss around $15.30 so my risk is only 30 cents a share against a $1.50 profit potential. I'm quite happy with that ratio.

Bullish flag

Bullish flags are some of the most reliable patterns, as long as your stock is in a strong trend before forming the flag.

A flag shows up when the trend pauses for a while and the share price trades in a tight range. It's called a flag because you can draw a rectangular box around it, like the shape of a flag. It might be moving upwards, downwards or sideways.

Bullish flags are only short term phenomena. One might last a few days or a couple of weeks. If you see what looks like a flag but the share price starts trading up and down in the range, it's formed a *channel*, which we already looked at and which is a longer term pattern. Note that flag patterns usually run in the opposite direction to the trend (imagine the center bar in the letter N).

Bullish flags are very quantifiable. The depth of the 'flag' which on the left I've shown here as x can be added to the breakout price to get your target share price. You'll enter a little above the line to make sure it's not a fake-out. And the stop-loss is just below the bottom line. (Just below, because some traders will try to "take out" the bulls by pushing the price just below the line before the price goes up again, so if you put your stop-loss actually on the line, you could lose what's actually a good trade. Taking a tiny bit more risk will deliver very significantly more return.)

Bullish pennant

Bullish pennants are the short term version of a triangle. The pennant is triangular, and they are both short-term signals. They typically don't last much longer than 10-15 days - 20 at the outside.

The pennant will form, typically after a big and fairly quick (steep) move in the price (which you see on the left). You'll then see prices consolidate into the pennant. You'll probably see this happen on lower volume, so it's worth checking the volume indicators for confirmation.

Now the thing that I particularly like about bullish flags and pennants is that when there's a breakout, it's a big one. They basically show the market taking a breather and drinking a Redbull before starting that uptrend again, and the uptrend is likely to be fast and furious.

Occasionally there will be a fake-out, so put a stop-loss just below the bottom line of the pennant. Meanwhile, your profit objective is the height of the 'mast' - the last strong move before the pennant started forming. So both your downside and your upside with this trade are easily quantifiable, and your upside will be significantly greater than the downside.

Look at the chart again and you'll see how I measured the height of the pennant where the pattern began, 'x', and then I've added this to the resistance line at the top of the pennant to give me my target price. I've shown you where I entered the trade, after the breakout, and where I would put a stop-loss.

Do remember that the target is an initial target. I won't necessarily sell at that point - I will take another look at the chart and reassess. If it looks as if the uptrend will continue, I'll set a new target and a new stop-loss. (The stop-loss is very important.) And maybe I will sell enough to cover my original stake, so my initial capital is recouped and all that's now at risk is the profit. But remember: winners run their wins, and only cut their losses, so I'm not going to be too cautious.

By the way, if you're still unsure on bullish flag and pennants, I would definitely suggest you watch my free bonus #1 companion masterclass because in Class 3 I demonstrate examples of both patterns with real life charts — which will hopefully help your learning!

Bullish falling wedge

Wedges are a bit of a refinement on the triangle. The market consolidates between two falling lines, with lower highs and lower lows. Both the support and resistance lines point downwards, but the resistance line is steeper, so you have what looks like the point of a pencil pointing downwards towards the right.

BULLISH FALLING WEDGE

So it's not like the pennant which is pretty much even on both sides, and pointing straight forwards - I find it easiest to spot the difference not by looking at the individual trendlines, but by seeing where the formation is telling me to look.

If a pennant was a pointing finger, it would be pointing along the road (to the right), whereas a wedge is pointing at a plane (if its a bearish rising wedge) or pointing at the pavement (if its a bullish falling wedge).

Confirmation for the wedge also comes from volume indicators, as generally, there is less and less volume traded as the wedge develops.

Perhaps it's counterintuitive, but a *falling* wedge heralds a price break *upwards*. The pointing finger is showing you the *reverse* of the real movement! However, look at the downward price moves inside the wedge and you'll understand why - they are getting shorter and shorter, the price is falling a bit less each time.

By the way, make sure you really are looking at a wedge - it should definitely show convergence (lines moving closer together). If the lines are nearer parallel, it may be establishing a channel, and that's an entirely different thing.

Not all wedges end in a breakout. That's one reason you might want to wait till you see the actual breakout before placing a trade. If it's a genuine breakout, not a fake-out, you'll see rising volume as the price goes up, too, though it *may* retest the top line of the wedge. (Remember, when the price breaks through a resistance line, that line becomes the new support.) Some traders will actually wait for that retest before buying - the problem, of course, is that they will possibly miss the fastest and most profitable breakouts.

To calculate potential profit, look at the successive lower highs within the wedge. Each of those highs represents a potential resistance point. So if the breakout happens at $40 and the last high was $46, you have a potential $6 profit. If things are still going well at that point, you can hang on in and wait for the next resistance level. Some moves go back to the initial price at which the wedge started. But every time you decide to stay in the trade, raise your stop-loss to just below the new support level.

Bearish flag

It will not surprise you to know that these are just the reverse of a bull flag - a consolidation phase in a strong downtrend.

Here's a bear flag. It's a small pattern in a downtrend making a rectangle, and you're looking for the breakout.

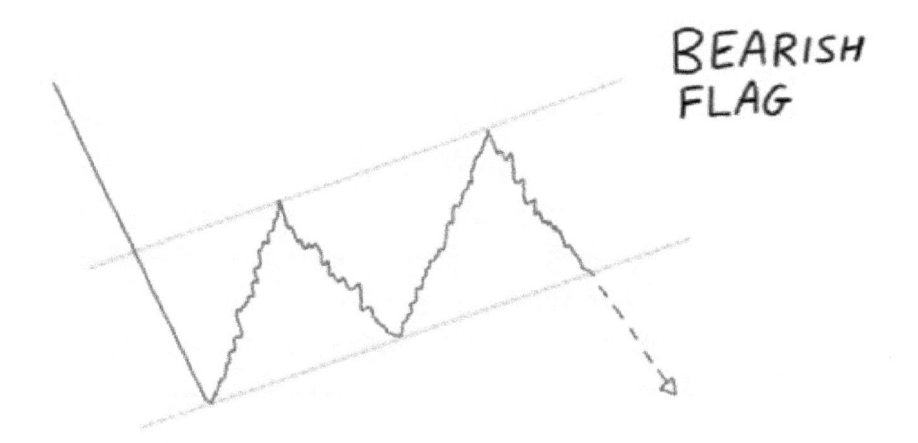

BEARISH FLAG

Bearish pennant

Here's a bear pennant. It's a small triangular formation and again, you're looking for that breakout that brings you back into the downtrend.

If you go short, you can capitalize on the big downwards move at the breakdown - but place a buy stop-limit order as a stop-loss just above the top line of the pennant, just in case.

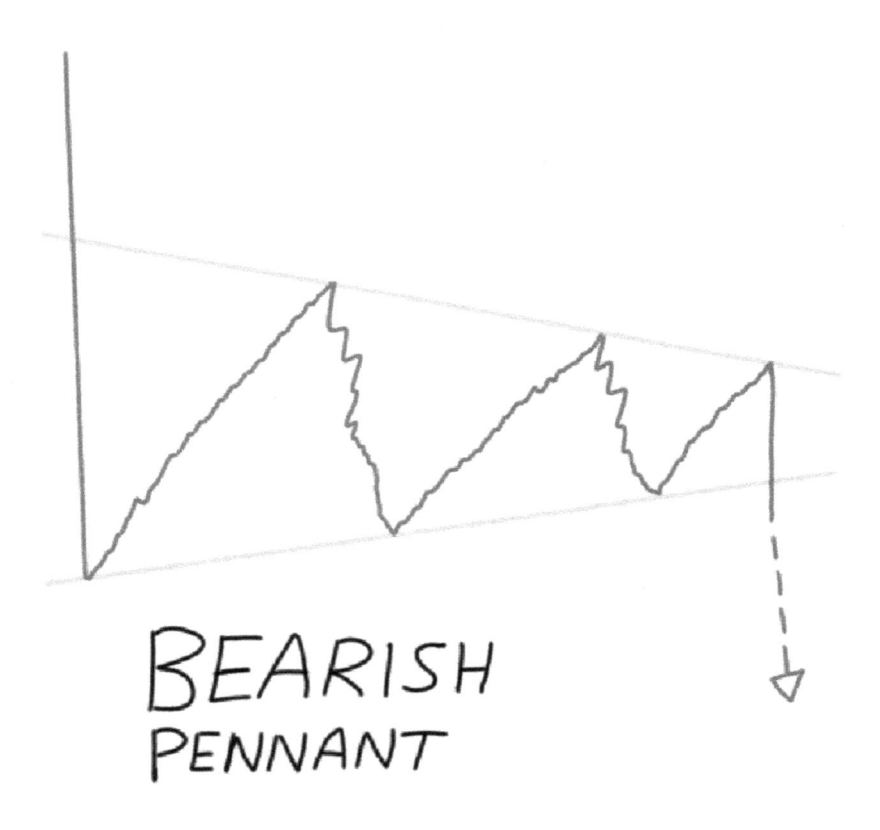

Below is a good chart example of a bearish pennant - Exide entered a downtrend late 2018, after what looks to me like a classic head and shoulders pattern (we'll look at those next chapter), but then look, it forms this upwards pennant in August 2019. Every time it gets to that bottom line there's the potential for a breakthrough, and look how fast it is when it comes. From $185 to $130 really, really fast. But of course, the price might have moved back up towards the top of the pennant one more time - even twice; so that's why you don't trade a pennant till the price has actually closed below the line.

In fact, you can spot quite a few different patterns in this chart- there's an uptrend from the beginning of the period to about October 2019, which I drew a line for. Also, I haven't drawn a line but perhaps you'd like to try to do so for the head-and-shoulders that forms between about April 2018 and April 2019. And then I have drawn a line for the downtrend, as well as for the bearish pennant pattern we already discussed.

Of course, it's easy to see all these patterns in hindsight. Would you have known what to do every time? Where would you have put your target price and your stop-losses? It's worth thinking about this every time you look at one of these charts.

Bearish and rising wedge

Remember that, counter-intuitively, a falling wedge leads to an upwards trend? A bearish wedge is one that is rising - and will probably lead to a breakdown. Apart from the fact that you'll have to trade short to capitalize on it, a bearish wedge works pretty much the same way as a bullish wedge.

BEARISH RISING WEDGE

The stock should be in a long term downtrend. The wedge is pointing upwards (like the analogy I gave of pointing to a plane). And the break will be downwards. Because of the risk of going short, you need to be very certain with this wedge - check the oscillators, as those should provide confirmation. If they don't, rethink!

Problems with continuation patterns

Continuation patterns are not always reliable. Sometimes they in fact end in a reversal - something you may pick up by looking at other indicators, such as RSI or OBV. If a rising wedge occurs when a stock is in an uptrend, it could potentially be a reversal signal leading to a downtrend - the breakout will still be on the downside.

Another problem with these patterns is that they are often tested by false breakouts, which can lose you money if you get tempted to take too many trades or don't set a close enough stop-loss. If you are trading continuation patterns a lot, keep a good record of your trades and their success rate per pattern. That will help you understand which patterns and trading methods are working best for you. Depending on your particular trading style, that might not be the same patterns and methods that work for me or anyone else.

Chapter 5 Quiz

1. For a pennant to give a strong signal
    a) The share price should already be in a defined trend
    b) The pennant should be long and thin
    c) The moving average should be underneath the pennant

2. What's the importance of the 'handle' in setting your stop-loss in a cup-and-handle trade?
    a) None
    b) You should set a stop-loss at a swing low within the handle or at the depth of the handle
    c) You should set a stop-loss way below the handle

3. What is a dead cat bounce?
    a) Cruelty to animals
    b) A temporary reversal in a long term trend
    c) A form of flag pattern that fails

4. Ascending and descending triangles are
    a) Good patterns to trade
    b) Not very useful
    c) Totally subjective

5. A wedge
    a) Always ends in a breakout
    b) Never ends in a breakout
    c) Ends in a breakout if there's good volume towards the end of the wedge.

A.Z Penn

6

Chapter 6: Reversal Patterns

Just as we saw that there were patterns that usually end in a continuation of the price trend, there are also many patterns that often lead to a reversal of the trend. This is where to borrow a phrase I've used before in this book; you find out that it may be a trend, but it's gonna bend!

Obviously with a reversal pattern it's going to be either at the top or the bottom of the market - for the foreseeable future anyway. At the top, you have what's called a *distribution* pattern - investors and traders who own the stock are deciding to sell (distribute) it, and eventually there are more sellers than buyers. At the bottom, you have an *accumulation* pattern as market participants begin to accumulate the stock, and the power moves to buyers from sellers.

You *cannot* have a reversal pattern without a preceding trend. There has to be something for it to reverse. If you're in any doubt about what looks like a reversal pattern, just set the chart for a longer time period and check that the trend is there and firmly established before the pattern starts to form.

As with continuation patterns, reversal patterns can fail, so watch them carefully for the breakout and place your stop-losses sensibly. You'll also find that the longer a pattern takes to develop, the larger the move is likely to be once it does break out, so patience is a virtue if you're trading these patterns.

Bump and Run Reversal Bottom

Remember the cup and handle? This starts out looking a bit like it, with a pretty symmetrical dip forming a 'cup', but then it breaks out above the trendline. Other people have described it as looking like a frying pan, with the 'handle' out left, along the trendline.

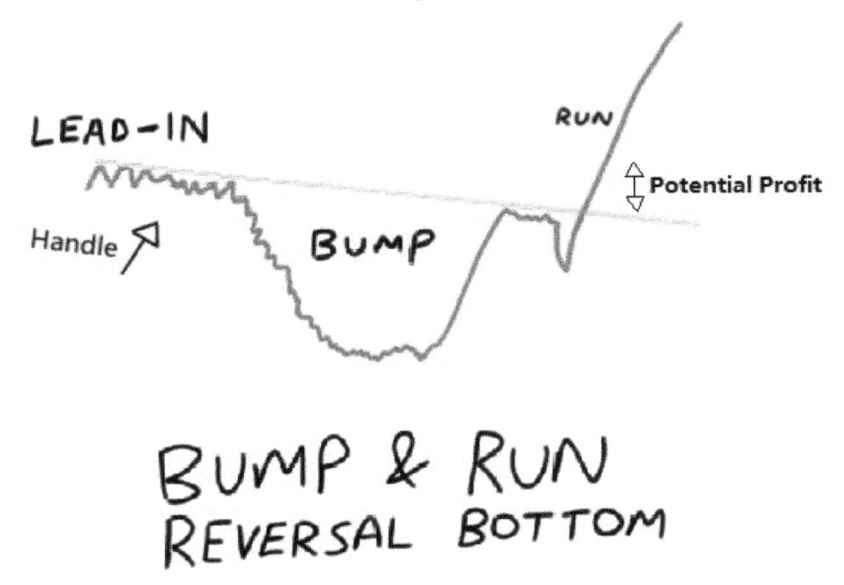

You'll find it in a downtrend, and you can draw the trendline along the downtrend - usually not a very steep one. It can take as much as a month for that trend to become established. Then you get the 'bump', cup, or frying pan, whatever you want to call it - the price drops quite steeply, then forms a nice round bottom, and starts climbing again. If the price closes above the trendline on the upside, it's a good buy signal, often signaling an upside of 50% or more.

This is a good quantifiable pattern, meaning that you can pretty much analyze how much upside you'll get out of the trade. If you mark the price at the top of the left 'handle', this is where normally you'd expect the price to rebound to if the bump and run makes a successful breakout. The bump (cup, frying pan) should normally be twice as deep as the handle, nicely defined, so you can see this pattern really clearly when it occurs.

And very often, the pattern delivers rather more than expected. So don't be too quick to sell - if the price is still running strongly upwards, supported for instance by high volume or by the MACD, use a trailing stop-loss and keep running your winner.

Tom Bulkowski discovered this trading pattern and according to him, it achieves its price target 76% of the time, with an average rise of 55%. That's a very good performance - most patterns have either a low success rate but high profitability, or a high success rate but lower profits. This one has both!

If you're a bit more daring and risk-friendly, you can also play this pattern by drawing parallel lines to the trendline, and buying on the way up when the price closes above one of those trendlines. How do you know how wide to make the trendlines? Simple - measure the highest to the lowest price in the handle, and that's your measurement for these trendlines. However, this trade doesn't have quite the success rate of waiting till the higher breakout, so you could get stopped out.

You may get a throwback, with the price falling back after the breakout. However, if you continue the main trendline, as long as the price doesn't close below the trendline, the breakout should still happen - you just need to wait for it. Only close the trade if the price falls below the trendline.

This is a really great trade for medium term long-only traders.

Bump and Run Reversal Top

Guess what? This is just the opposite of the Bump and Run Reversal Bottom. So it's a good trade for short traders.

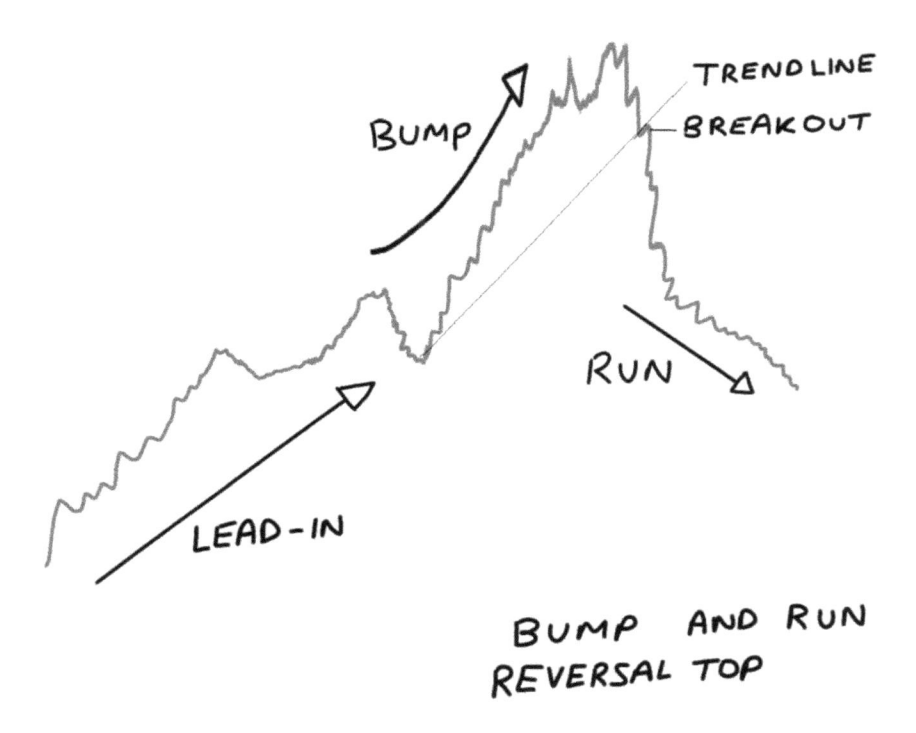

Let's just talk through how it works. The 'handle' or 'lead-in' sees quite an orderly trading, with the buyers setting the tone and the stock closing up most days in a fairly tight range. Then everyone notices the stock is doing well, and you get some people buying it because it's going up, speculating, more short-term traders getting into the market. Prices go up much more sharply and usually the volume increases, too - lots of traders jumping in.

And that's not sustainable. Right at the top you might get a double top, or just a very rounded top. And then people start getting cold feet. Some of the investors who held on to the stock all the way up the bump decide to take a profit. Some of the speculators who bought in right at the top are stop-lossed out. Others get scared and sell. And when the price breaks the trendline, you know that now things have got serious, and you go short.

As with the bump and run bottom, this pattern *can* see a retracement (temporary reversal). The retracement is rarely more than half the 'bump' size, but if you're trading short, you will be stopped out. Keep watching because if the price comes back to close below the trendline again, this is the real thing - and you should take that short again.

Another nice thing about bump and run? While it can take three or four months to set up the lead-in and the bump, the 'run' part of the pattern often takes just a few days to deliver you a significant profit, so your money is at risk for very little time. You just have to be patient watching the pattern and waiting for the right time.

Double and Triple Bottom

This is one of the first patterns I ever learned.

A double bottom looks like a letter 'W'. Up, down a bit, up a bit, and then down again. The psychology of it works like this: the price is trending down, with lots of sellers exiting the stock. Then a few speculators or maybe some value investors look at the price and think, "Hey, this is cheap," and buy in. But the price doesn't get very far. Sellers who missed their chance to get out earlier decide to sell, and some of the buyers look at the panic and think, "Okay, I'll take my profit before it goes down more". This selling drives the price back down - but only to where it was before, and now you have buyers again.

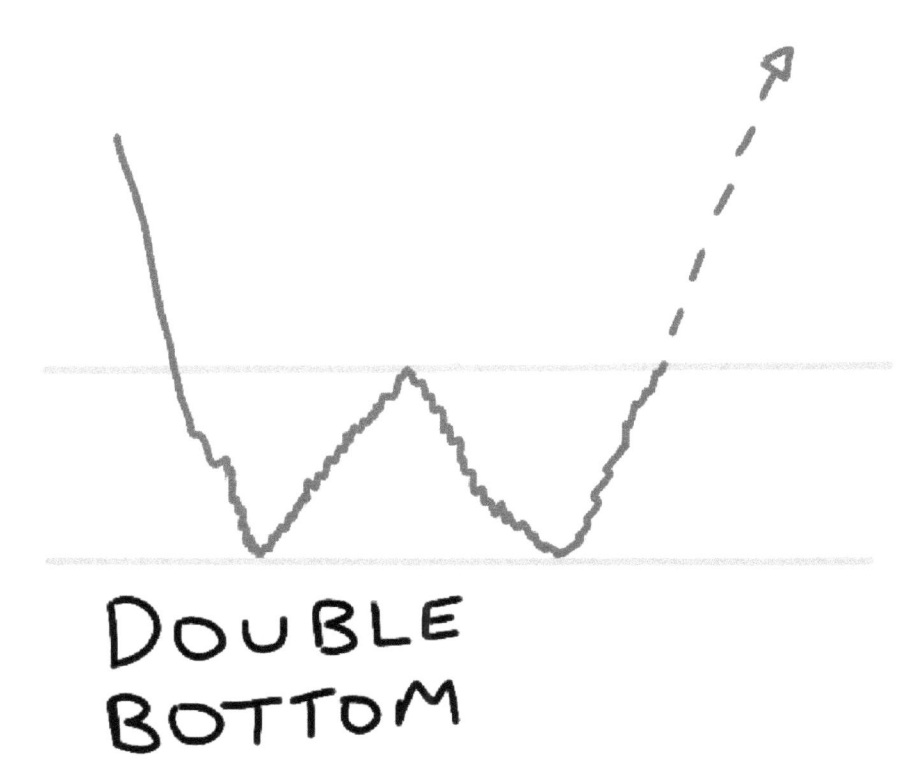

DOUBLE BOTTOM

Now, of course the price could bounce around between those levels for a while, and if it did, it would form a channel. But you have two lines that you can draw across that W now (as I've shown with the light blue lines). First of all, the failed bounce forms a resistance line, so you can draw a horizontal line at the top of the bounce. And secondly, the two bottom corners of the W form a support line. So you can draw a line between them, too.

If the price breaks through the resistance line and closes above it, it's a buy signal. You can also quantify how much profit you expect to make. Measure the move between the bottom corners and the failed bounce, and you can expect to make at least 60% and possibly 80% of that as a profit, and fairly quickly, too. Of course, you're going to put a stop-loss below the resistance line, so if it does turn out to be a fake-out, you don't lose too much.

I like this pattern because it has a high-profit potential. That said, you'll find that you 'kiss a lot of frogs' in terms of price action that looks like turning into a double bottom and doesn't.

All is not lost though, because the share price might be forming a *triple bottom*. (Yes, that is a share price reversal pattern and not a rare medical problem.) This behaves similarly to a double bottom, except that it takes longer to get round to breaking out. Your buying signal - the price closing above the resistance line at the top of the bounces - is the same, and your profit potential is the same.

Be smart, though. Your profit potential is big, but just in case it doesn't work out that way, remember to place a *trailing stop* which will ensure if the share price falls a certain percentage below the high, you will still get out at a profit.

Double and Triple Top

Okay, a double or triple top is just a double or triple bottom the other way round. The difference is that to make real money out of this one, you need to go short - that is, sell shares you don't own. Then when the price has gone down, you close the deal by buying shares at the lower price. Not all brokers will let you go short.

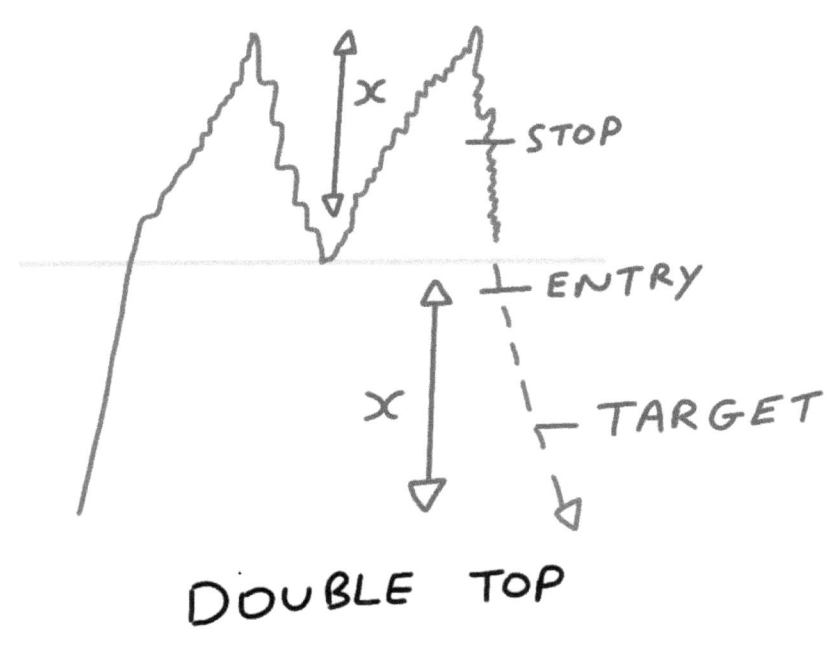

[Hand-drawn chart labeled "DOUBLE TOP" with annotations: STOP, ENTRY, TARGET]

But double and triple top formations are also interesting if you have a longer-term investment portfolio as well as your trading portfolio. I don't think it's a great idea to "time the market" by trying to sell at the highs and buy back at the lows, but if you see a top forming, you might want to take a few profits, lighten up your more speculative positions, and maybe take a little insurance out in the form of a put option or an inverse ETF (exchange traded fund).

- A put option gives you the right to sell a stock at a given price. If the stock is trading at $242 and you think it's going to fall, you could buy a put option at $180. Traded options have an expiry date. Usually, you won't hold it that long, just till your trade works out.

- While most ETFs reflect the performance of a market, an inverse ETF gives you the exact opposite. If the market goes up, the ETF goes down. What you're interested in as a short seller is that if the market goes down, the ETF goes UP. Buying an inverse ETF can make you money if you trade a good strong breakdown.

At the same time, as an equity investor, if I see a double bottom forming, I know it's time to look and see if I can buy some more of my favorite stocks at a good value.

The chart below shows Jan 2001-March 2004 of S&P 500 (The months and years are shown under the volume bars, not under the price chart, which is kind of annoying, but you should be able to follow them.)

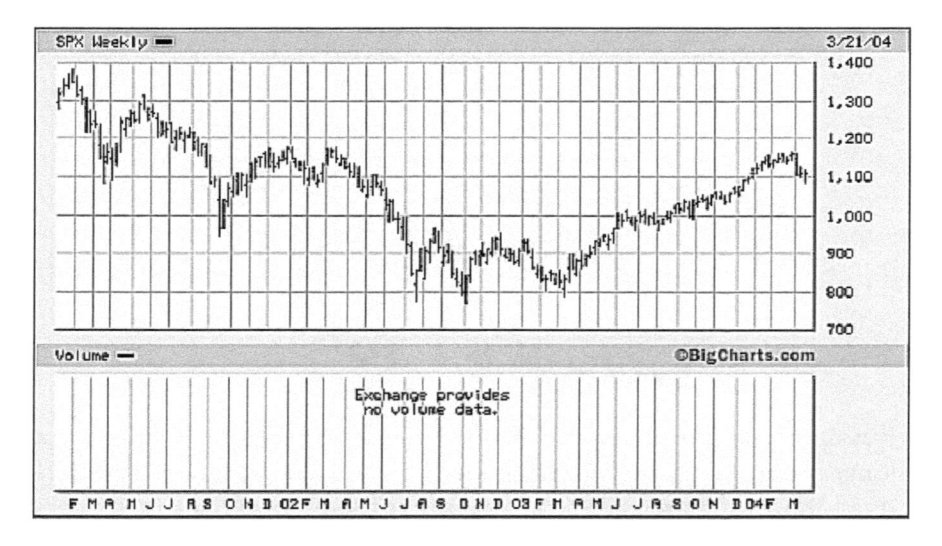

Look at how stocks come right off the top in 2001, there's a little retracement on the way down, but there's a clear double bottom in June and September 2002. You then see the price drop from about $1,000 to just below $800, then rises again, doesn't get much further than $950, then falls back. Then you have another failed breakout, you can see that resistance line at $950 holds, and the price comes back again - but it doesn't hit the support line, it turns before closing below $800 (there's just the little tail of the low below the line) and then it just keeps going up, fast to $1,000 and then all the way to $1,150.

By the way, sometimes you'll find a double bottom doesn't quite work out, but later, a second double bottom formation starts to show. Often, it will form with the same bottom, but the intermediate highs are lower than in the first pattern. This one could be the real deal, and with stronger resistance levels, when it breaks out, it could go up much faster than you'd expect. So never give up on your double bottoms! Keep following the chart to see what happens next!

And in fact, you might want to enter a limit order to buy just above the resistance line, so that if you're not trading all day, your broker will do the work for you. At the same time, enter your stop-loss order little way below the breakout level - always allow a little space, just in case there's a fake retracement. Here I would probably have thought about entering around $925 or a little higher, and probably I'd put a stop-loss around $880.

Head-and-Shoulders Top

First, I have to mention that this pattern has nothing to do with shampoo. What it does is to form a pattern a bit like a head-and-shoulders photo - a left shoulder, the 'head' in the middle, and a right shoulder.

If you want to trade this pattern, you need to go short - that is, either sell shares you don't have (so you need a broker who will let you go short), or use some other way of taking a risk on the price going *down*. When the shares hit your target, you make a purchase order, and buy the shares below the price you sold them. Neat.

You'll find this pattern coming after a strong uptrend. It's a medium to long term pattern - it's not going to play out in much less than a month. And if it's a real head and shoulders, you will see that after the higher 'head' formation, the share price will hit the 'neckline' already established between the left shoulder and the head, and bounce off it again. You can draw this neckline across the chart; it's usually pretty flat, but sometimes it has a slope. If it slopes downwards, it's particularly bearish.

So we now have a chart with three lines on it - the price, the trendline, and the neckline.

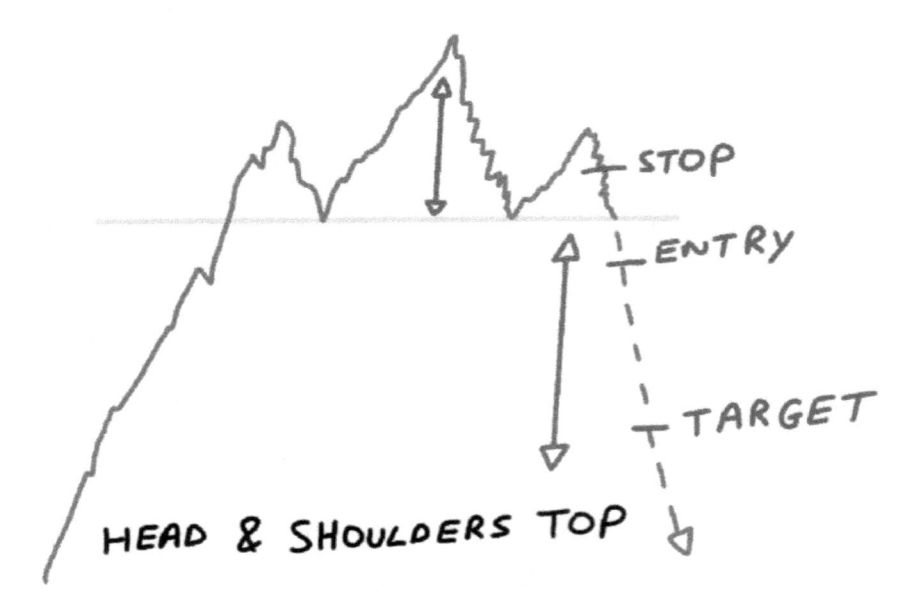

[Hand-drawn chart showing a Head & Shoulders Top pattern with labels: STOP, ENTRY, TARGET, and "HEAD & SHOULDERS TOP"]

The low of the left shoulder doesn't usually break the trendline. So the trend is intact till you get to the head. When the share price comes down again to the neckline, it does break the trendline. So that's (probably) the end of the uptrend, but it's not time to buy yet, because the neckline provides resistance and the price will bounce off it to form the right shoulder.

The moment you're looking for is when the price comes down again from the right shoulder. (Usually, though not always, the shoulders are roughly symmetrical.) Keep watching till it closes below the neckline. It has now gone through the resistance level and its time to go short. At this point, your profit target is the difference between the top of the head and the price at the neckline - subtract this from the current share price for your close-out price. So, for instance, if the price got to $58, the neckline is at $50, then my target profit is $8, and my target price is $50-8 = $42.

There can be a retracement up to the neckline, but if it doesn't breakthrough, the price will fall again. That's why you should probably set your stop-loss slightly *above* the neckline, allowing for that little bounce - you won't be stopped out of a profitable trade.

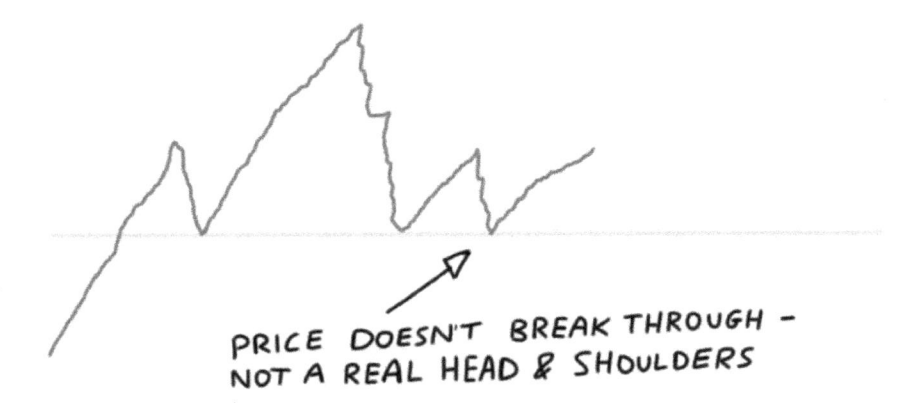

PRICE DOESN'T BREAK THROUGH - NOT A REAL HEAD & SHOULDERS

Note that if the price doesn't actually close below the neckline, it's not an actual head-and-shoulders top pattern. Look at the chart above and you can see what looked like the real thing - but wasn't.

Some traders set their stop-loss at the top of the right shoulder, but that's pretty loose and you could lose quite a bit if the reversal doesn't materialize.

Head-and-Shoulders Bottom

You've probably guessed that this is the opposite of a head-and-shoulders top. The difference is that it comes after a downtrend, so it's a reversal pattern that will have the stock soaring upwards afterwards.

Head and shoulders formations are not equal. Their profitability is affected by a couple of factors:
1. The taller the 'head' in relation to the neckline, the greater your trade's profit potential.
2. A smaller right shoulder shows the stock is already losing momentum and is less likely to bounce out of the reversal.

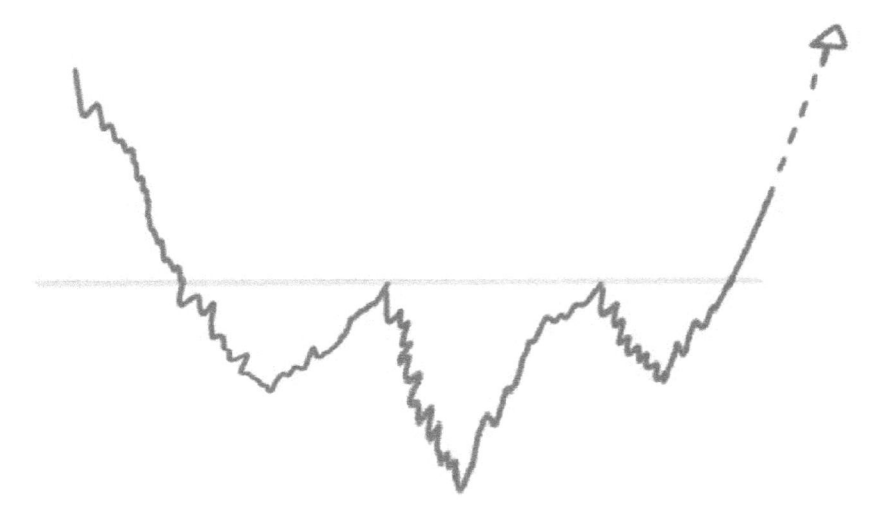

HEAD & SHOULDERS BOTTOM

You should also watch the volume of shares being traded. On a classic head and shoulders bottom pattern, the volume will increase and be really strong on the breakout. Strong volume tells you that the move is not a small correction, but a proper breakout with big funds behind it that should deliver you a good profit.

If the price is still dropping when you reach the target, don't get too greedy. It might be time to lighten up and take the risk out of your position by selling some of your shares, even if you don't sell the whole position. Take a good look at the chart before you make your decision, and in particular, look at the momentum indicators - if they're strong, you might be in for the ride, but if it seems like momentum is falling, it's time to exit your trade and book your profit.

Rounding Bottom/Saucer

We talked about the cup and handle formation, but the rounding bottom is just a cup. No handle. It comes when an existing downtrend slows down, bounces around, and creates a rounded trough with a flattish bottom. Quite a few chartists call this a 'saucer', as it is, usually, a bit flatter than a cup.

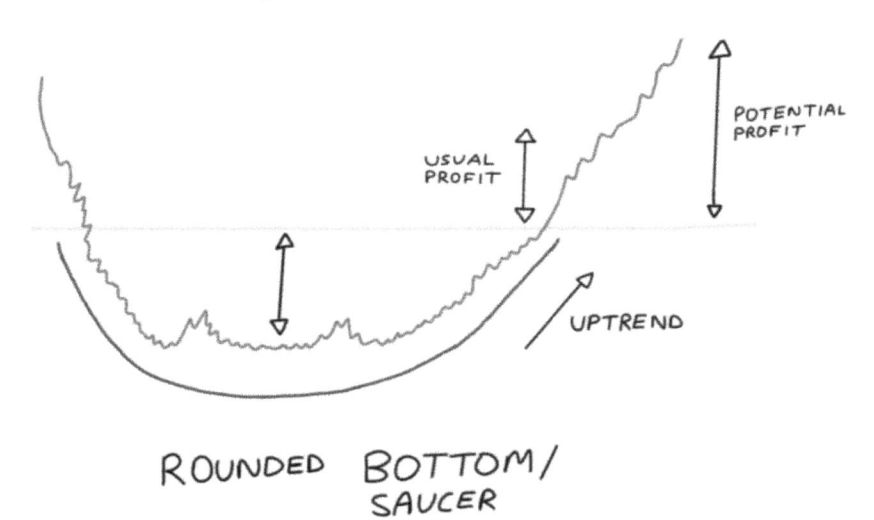

ROUNDED BOTTOM/SAUCER

Drawing the neckline isn't quite as easy as with the preceding patterns. You're looking for the last proper price spike before the saucer started to form. This is one of these times that charting can be an art rather than a science; there could be several places looking equally possible, but most of the time, there will be one spike just a little more pronounced than the others. So get your ruler, or the crosshairs on your trading screen, find the spike and then draw horizontally across the whole chart so that the line crosses the top of the spike. Then you just have to watch till the price closes above the line, and buy.

It's also tricky to plot your target profitability. It's probably best to take about half the depth of the 'saucer' and then add that to the neckline - in about a third of cases the pattern captures the whole depth of the 'saucer' as profit, but you can't depend on that. So this pattern is more limited in profitability than other reversals, but to make for that it is quite reliable. I've shown both levels of profit target on the chart.

The price may retrace at the neckline before breaking through. But this is a pattern with a nearly 60% success rate if you get it right. The flatter the saucer, the more likely you are to get a good fast breakout. If you track volume, the volume indicators should follow the pattern of the saucer - high at the beginning of the decline, low in the middle where the price is drifting along, and then increasing as the price starts to go up again. That's a good confirmation for your trade.

This chart comes from tradingview.com, another source of charting, with a thriving community - one of the members suggested the gold price was forming a rounding bottom. It actually makes the point about the 'spike' much better than our drawing - you can see there are two highs before the bottom starts to form, and the neckline is drawn across from the second one. After that, we're definitely in the rounding bottom. But you *might* have seen the little spike that goes above the neckline, a bit earlier, as the beginning of the bottom, in which case you would just get into the trade a bit higher. (You can sign up for a free trial on TradingView if you're interested; it covers commodities, currencies and cryptos as well as equities.)

Where do you put your stop-loss? There's no really obvious place. Some traders put it at the midpoint of the saucer - that is, halfway up - but that only gives you a 1:1 risk:reward ratio. I prefer to put it just below the breakout, and I know another trader who puts it at the bottom of the breakout candle (yes, you have to use a candlestick chart to do that).

Like other reversal patterns, this can be quite a long term pattern. It's not for day traders, but if you're looking to trade positions and hold them for several months, this can be a useful pattern to look for.

Parabolic Rise or Run-Up

If you have done math to a high level, you know what a parabola is. If you ever played frisbee, you probably have quite a good idea. If not, I'm going to have to explain what 'parabolic' means before we start discussing the pattern.

A parabola is a plane curve which is mirror-symmetrical. Okay, if that doesn't mean much, let's try to make it easier. Imagine you have an ice cream cone. If you cut through it horizontally, you'd get a circle. If you cut through it on the skew, you'd get an oval or ellipse. If you cut through it from somewhere on the side to halfway through the top, you'd have a parabola - a kind of long thin curve. You would also have wasted a lot of ice cream.

I fully accept that this is not one of my most talented drawings, and I am no Michelangelo, but I hope you now have a good idea of what a parabola looks like!

You don't get to see the whole parabola in this reversal pattern, only half of it. And you see it upside down, like half a letter 'U'. There are two things to notice about this curve and that gives us two ways to trade it.

1. It's a bit like a series of steps, if you look at the candlesticks - particularly since on a candlestick chart each 'step' has one big, bullish candlestick at the start of it. Every time the price hits a high, it should be higher than the previous high, and the low in between should be higher than the previous low.
2. But the second thing that you really have to notice is that the curve keeps getting steeper and steeper. And there is a limit to how far that can go.

Short term traders often trade their way up the 'staircase' either using moving averages (buying when the price moves up through the moving average), or using flags and pennants, which we looked at in the chapter on continuation patterns.

But if the curve continues to steepen, at a certain point it's going up almost vertically. If you continued to draw the curve, it would have to go back in time, which is obviously impossible. People are buying like there's no tomorrow - people are buying in a panic because "if you don't buy it now, you'll never be able to get into the stock". They have FOMO big time. There is a bubble mentality.

Here's GameStop - it's not quite a classic 'staircase' though if you look at the candlesticks, the jagged price line in black and red on the chart, you can see a big candle starts one step up about 22nd December, and then there's another big step up around 14th January. And then there's another about the 24th January, and at this point, the curve has really steepened. Look back to the previous year and you'll see how the trend was running at an angle of about 20 degrees, maybe, and suddenly it's almost vertical.

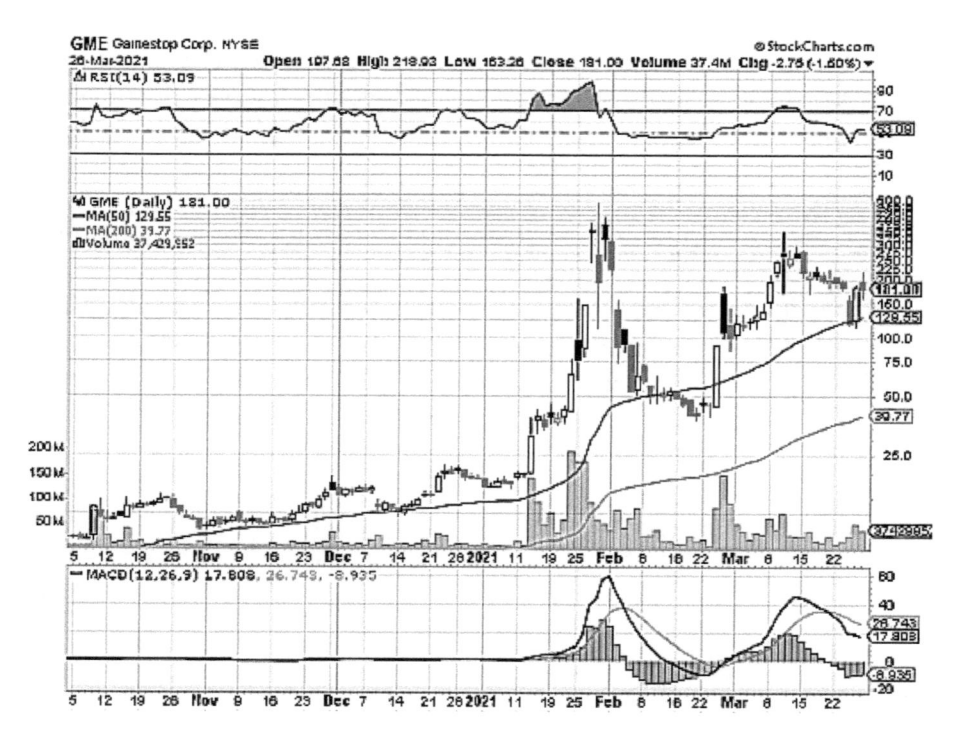

You *could* try to trade that steep vertical. Plenty of small investors did. For those who got out at the top, great. (And by the way, thiss chart also illustrates why going short is dangerous. Plenty of hedge fund managers would short GameStop for very good reasons. And they were *bleeding* money.)

Those who had been in GameStop since 2020 were fine too; maybe feeling a bit miserable that they weren't multi-millionaires anymore, but just ordinary common or garden millionaires, but hey, that's not so bad. But the little guys who bought in because they read about it in the press or on Reddit and got caught up in the excitement - they were toast, with a capital T.

Where do you go short? You have to draw a trendline using successive lows. When the stock price goes south through the trendline, catch the break. Weakening momentum oscillators might also confirm the trade.

Your target profit? Quite often, the share price will go all the way back to the beginning of the really steep part of the curve. And that's exactly what happened with GameStop in mid-February.

But you have to be careful with this one. Set a really tight stop-loss. Sometimes you get one or two big swings at the top. In fact, this is a lovely reversal to play as a day trader; I don't particularly like it, even though the potential rewards are very high, and if I do play this kind of curve, I don't keep my position open overnight. I'm just there to catch those big moves down, and as you can see, there were some very big moves indeed.

The other reason to be careful - look at the volume bars in that chart during late January. There's an awful lot of stock being traded; emotions are very high, some people are facing huge margin calls from their brokers. It's a very tough market to trade in.

Now you know both continuation patterns and reversal patterns. You can guess whether the stock will carry on in its current trend, or break out and reverse. We've talked about how to trade the patterns, and - an important factor - where to put stop-losses so you don't lose your shirt.

Most of these patterns are medium to long term. But in the next chapter, I'm going to take a look at patterns that are sometimes useful in the really short term - candlesticks. And this Japanese technique is a whole new ball game.

Chapter 6 Quiz

1. If a double bottom fails, and becomes a triple bottom instead, my target price and stop-loss will be
    a) Half what I expected
    b) Exactly the same
    c) You don't trade triple bottoms

2. When you have a parabolic rise, you'd expect trading volume to be
    a) Low
    b) Normal
    c) Extremely high

3. The flatter the saucer,
    a) The faster the breakout
    b) The less likely it is to be a signal
    c) The more likely you are to spill your tea

4. Reversal patterns usually
    a) Take longer to set up than they do to break out
    b) Don't happen when the market is in an uptrend
    c) Are exactly symmetrical

5. The Bump and run reversal is
    a) Only for day traders
    b) A good trade for medium term long-only traders
    c) Almost never profitable
    d) A bad car accident

A.Z Penn

7

Chapter 7: 16 Candlestick Patterns that Every Trader Should Know

So far, we've been looking at western style price charts and even where there are candlesticks, we've been looking at them over such a long period that we're looking at trends rather than individual time periods. But candlestick charts give you lots of information besides the trend - in the shape of the candlesticks and in particular very short term formations, maybe just a couple of days.

So this chapter is about candlesticks, and looking at the patterns that are really useful. There are six bullish patterns, six bearish patterns, and four continuation patterns - and if you didn't enjoy all that jargon in the chapter on indicators (RSI, OBV, MACD, ODX), I can promise you will find the names of the different candlestick patterns much more user-friendly and even on occasion quite humorous.

So what is a candlestick?

A candlestick is slightly different from the OHLC line that most charts show. It was developed in the Japanese rice market and it shows pretty much the same information, but in a format that emphasizes different facets of the share price movement.

The open-to-close range is represented in a big fat *body*. This has a different color depending on whether the share price went up or down.
- UP used to have an open white body with black outlines in old-fashioned charts, but now we have a full-color pixelated world; it might also be green.
- DOWN used to be an all-black body, but nowadays it's often red. Think of funerals, or think of red lights - the message is the same.

The body is the first thing you see, but you will also see little lines sticking out from one or both ends. Some traders call them the *wick*, other traders call it the original Japanese term, *shadow*. These show the intra-day high and/or low. If the day closed at the high, there is no upper shadow; if it closed at the low, there is no lower shadow.

I'm using my hand-drawn slides again. Remember green = up, red = down. A bit like traffic lights where green = go, red = stop. But if you ever look at older books on charting, you'll see the upwards candle as white and the downwards one shaded black.

(Just to refresh your memory: if the day closed at the high, what color is the body? If it closed at the low?)

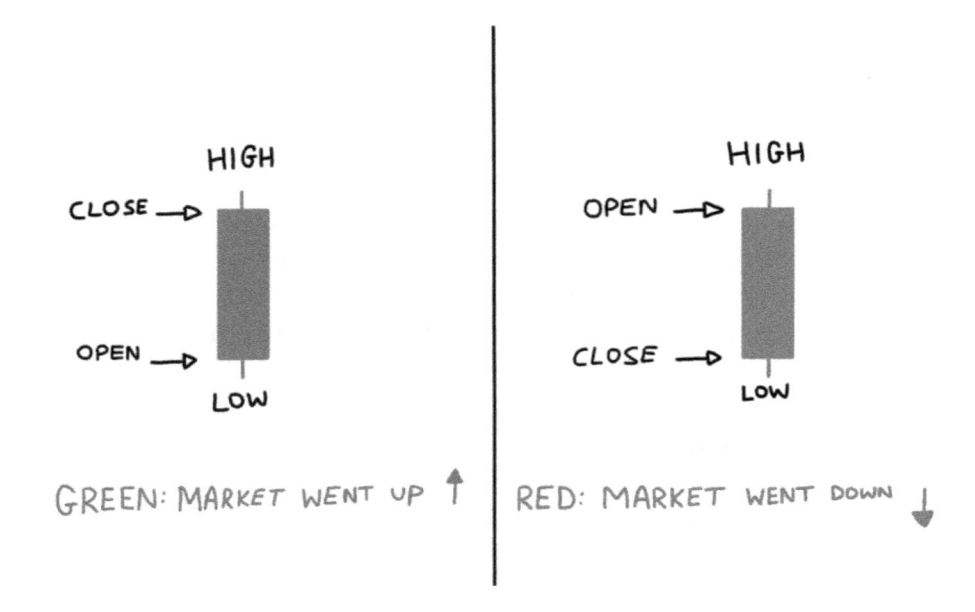

So a great tall green-bodied candlestick with no top shadow and a short bottom shadow means the stock rose nearly all day, only dipped a really tiny amount below the open in trading, and then closed at a high. A short stubby red candlestick with a long bottom shadow and a short top shadow shows that the price closed the day not far from where it started, but after some big selling action pushed the price down - and that it never traded very far above the opening price.

Try drawing some candlesticks for yourself on a bit of paper and think about what they mean.

Now let's look at a few candlestick patterns. They can be a single candlestick on its own, or a series of candlesticks.

Six Bullish Candlestick Patterns

1. Hammer

The hammer looks like a hammer, with the head up. It has a short green body, no (or almost no) upper shadow and a long lower shadow. So that means the stock traded up (the green body), but didn't close far from where it started (the small body), but it went way down during the day (the long shadow) before closing up. This was a battle between bulls and bears, and the bulls won.

Very often, the hammer comes after a short downtrend, and it's a sign the trend will reverse, and the stock price will start to go up.

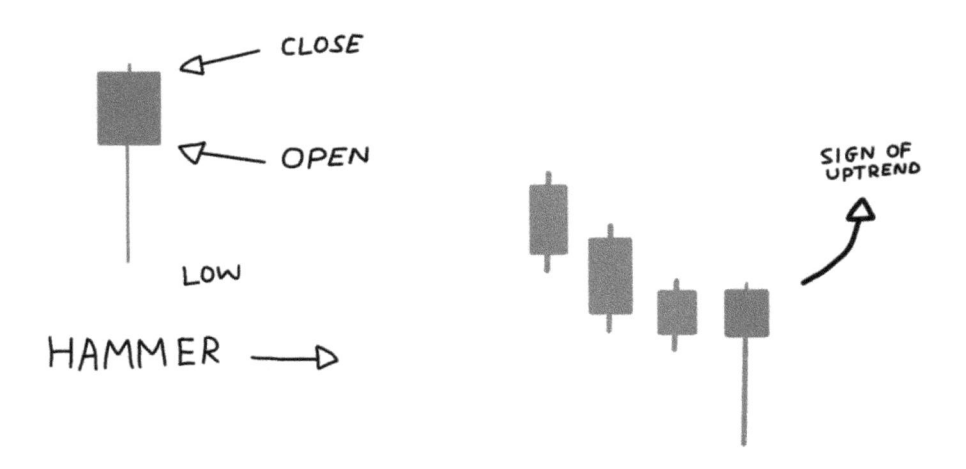

2. Inverse Hammer

The only difference with the inverse hammer is that it's hanging upside down - a short green body (the hammerhead) with a tall upper shadow and much shorter or no lower shadow. So here, the battle went a different way - the bulls tried to push the price up, the bears managed to push it down again, but the bears still lost, because the price ended up on the day. So again, it's a sign that the market could be set to go up in the near term.

Sometimes, you get two almost identical candles together at the top of an uptrend, though - a green and then red. That's an inverse hammer and then a shooting star, and this combination is called a 'tweezer top'. It indicates that a reversal is imminent and the market is likely to turn down. You can also have a tweezer bottom - just the reverse, showing the reversal is on its way and things should start moving up.

I should say I like the tweezers a lot. I've found them one of the easiest candlestick patterns to see, and they're also pretty reliable.

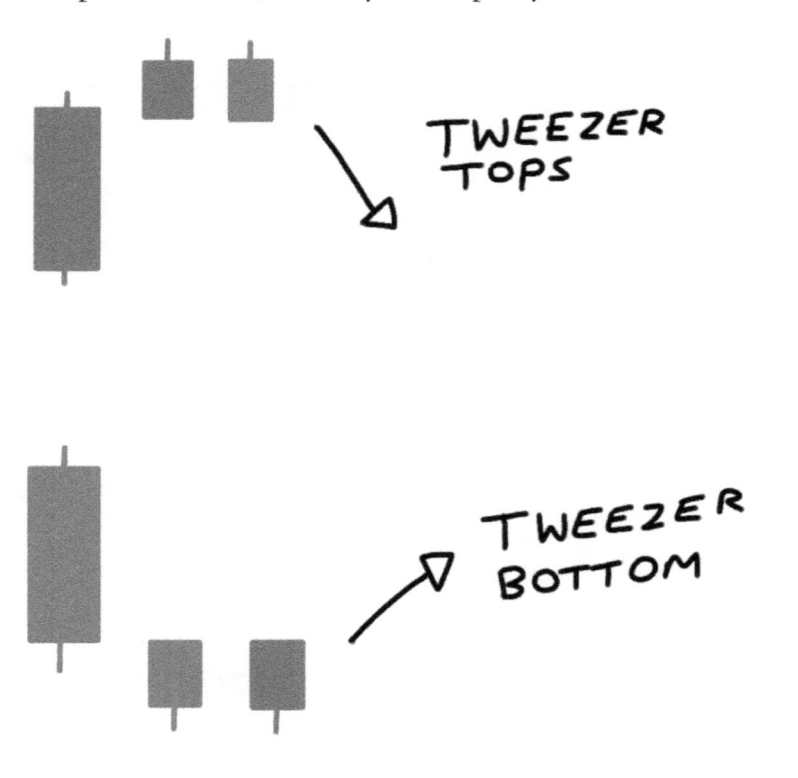

3. Bullish Engulfing

This has a small red candlestick that is completely 'engulfed' by the big green candle that follows it. The bottom of the green candlestick is either equal to or lower than the red, showing the share price opened at the same level or lower, but the price has really moved up and closed the day much higher. A victory for the bulls!

Again, bullish engulfing is usually a reversal pattern in a downtrend.

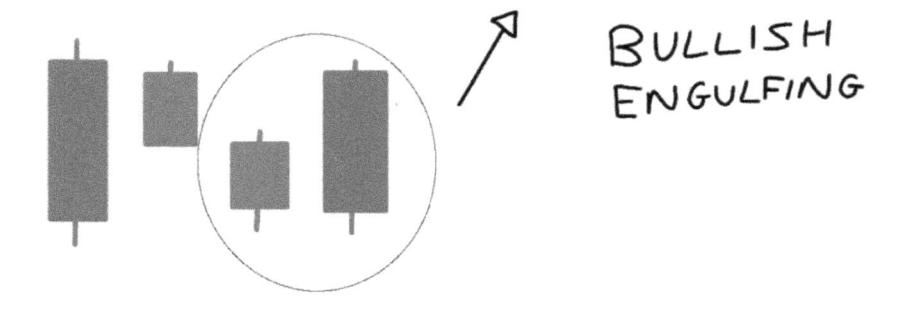

4. Piercing Line

The first step with the Piercing Line is to find two big candles, a red one followed by a green one. They both need to be good long candles.

Now you need to look at their relationship. The green should be lower than the red - so that means the price opened lower than the day before, but rose during the day.

Next, you need to look at how far up the price managed to get. It needs to have closed more than halfway up the red bar. If it nearly got to the top of the red bar, that's a really strong signal. The downtrend should reverse.

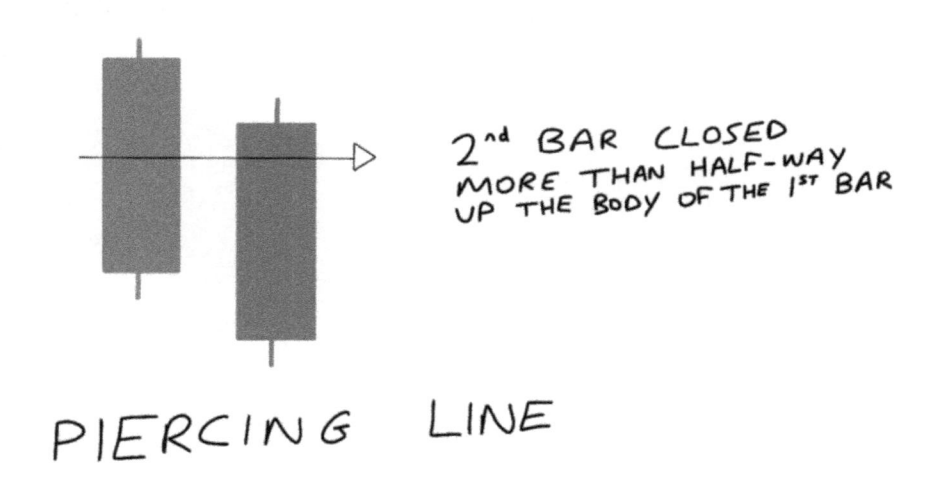

2nd BAR CLOSED MORE THAN HALF-WAY UP THE BODY OF THE 1ST BAR

PIERCING LINE

5. Morning Star

Morning Star happens in a big downtrend and it is a sign of hope that the night will soon be over and the morning should be coming. We've had one-stick and two-stick patterns; this is a three-stick pattern, a small candle squashed in between two long ones. The first long candle is red, and the second one green - the end of the downtrend with a low close, and the beginning of the uptrend with a high close.

Imagine a 'star' between two mountains if you need help remembering this one. The best morning star pattern is where there's no crossover at all between the star's body and the bodies of the other two candlesticks (it doesn't matter if the shadows overlap). In other words, trading gapped down before the star, and gapped up after the star. That's a good bullish signal.

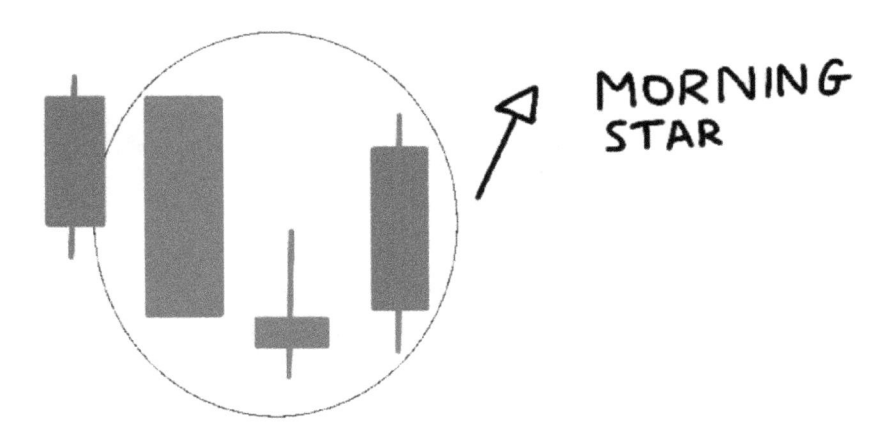

MORNING STAR

6. Three White Soldiers

Of course, nowadays this could be three green soldiers! It's another three-stick pattern, with three white or green candles marching uphill. They should, to form a really good signal, have short shadows. (Think about that; the price hardly fell or didn't fall at all below the open, and it closed near the high. So the bulls in the market, the buyers, had life all their own way.)

Three white soldiers are easy to spot because the candlesticks are long ones, and contrast with generally smaller and mainly red candlesticks in the run-up to the signal. It's a really strong bullish signal and definitely worth trading.

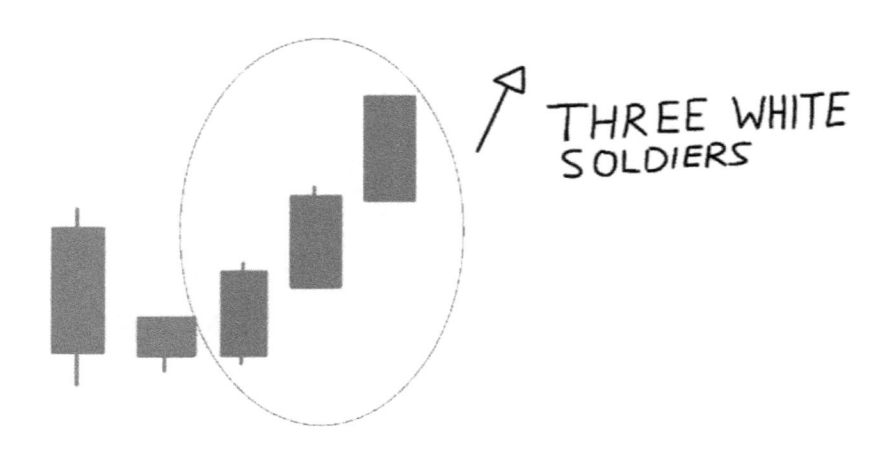

Six Bearish Candlestick Patterns

1. Hanging Man

It would be quite easy to confuse the hanging man with the hammer. But the hanging man is red, with a big downside shadow. The day saw a big sell-off, and even though buyers got the price back up again, it was still down on the day.

Hanging Man is a reversal pattern. You'll find him 'hung up high', at the top of an uptrend, and he tells you prices are going to start going down. I mean, with a name like Hanging Man, you wouldn't expect it to be good news, would you? Again this helps us to identify him, because the hammer comes within a downtrend.

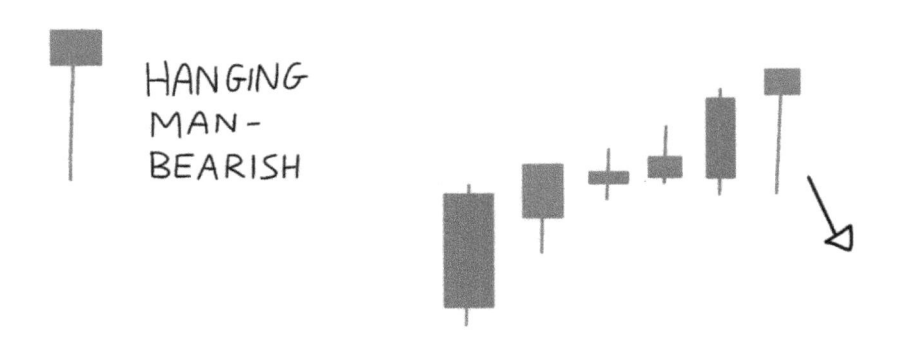

HANGING MAN - BEARISH

2. Shooting Star

This is quite like the inverted hammer. It comes at the top of an uptrend, and you'll see it has a tiny body and a really long shadow or wick at the top. And while the inverted hammer is green, this is red - it's a warning sign. (If you find the shooting star followed by an inverted hammer that looks almost exactly the same, though, you have 'tweezer bottoms', which sounds rather painful but is a good reversal pattern showing the market is likely to rise out of a downtrend.)

Let's explain what's going on when you see a shooting star. It gapped up, so the opening was just above the day before's close, and it went way up to the high but then came all the way - or almost all the way - back down again. And now here we are with the next candlestick gapping down; that's all we need to know. The new trend will be downwards.

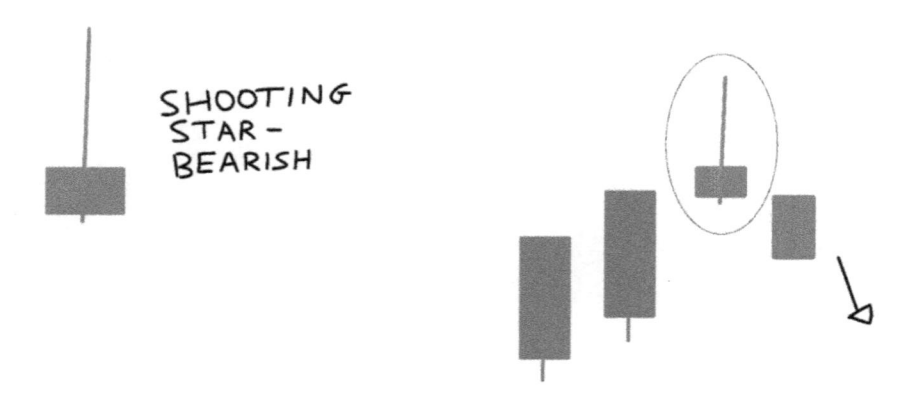

SHOOTING STAR - BEARISH

3. Bearish Engulfing

This is the other way around from the bullish engulfing. The first candle is a little green one, and the second is a big red one. The upwards movement has stalled, and the downtrend begins with a big move down.

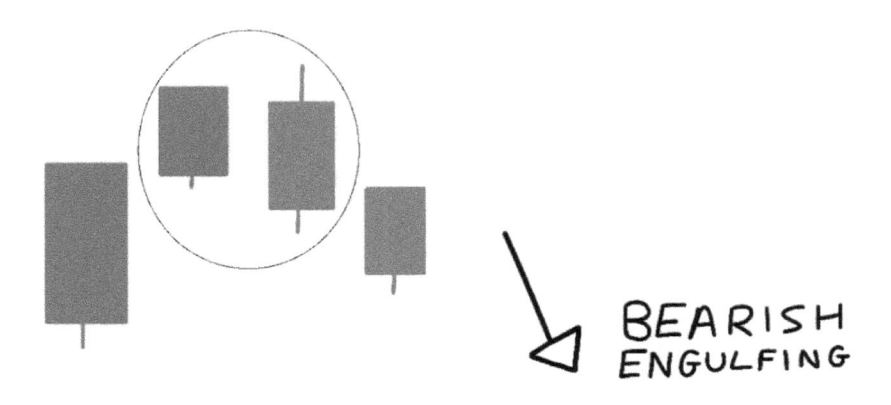

4. Evening Star

The evening star is the reverse of the morning star; it tells you night is only just beginning.

It's three candles, just like a morning star; two big candles sandwiching the tiny one in the middle. First a big green one, then a little green one with hardly any body, like a twinkling star, and then the big red candlestick which tells you all you need to know. We're going down, down, down.

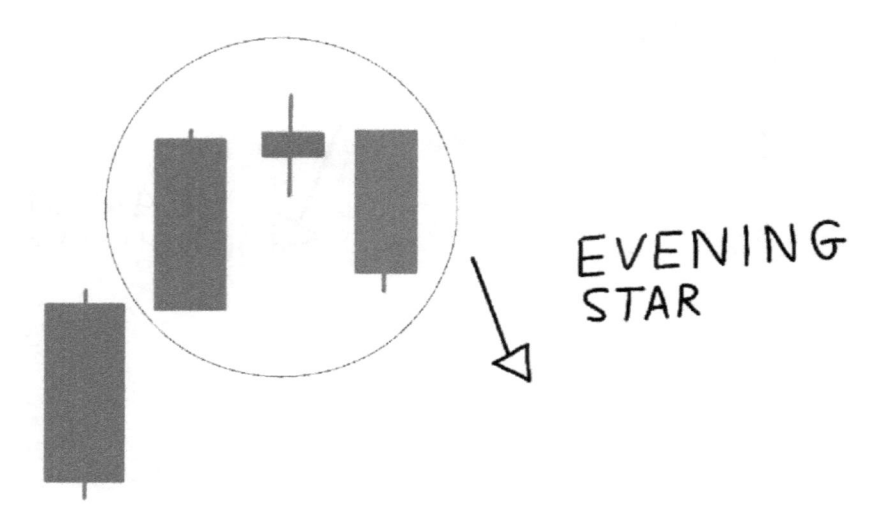

5. Three Black Crows

Three white soldiers showed you the market was going up. Three black crows are just the reverse. There are three big long black (or red) candlesticks in a row, each lower than the other. And you guessed it, they are not good news. (Unless you're short, of course.) The price is going to head downwards.

The only problem with recognizing the Three Black Crows is that nowadays they're quite likely to be red.

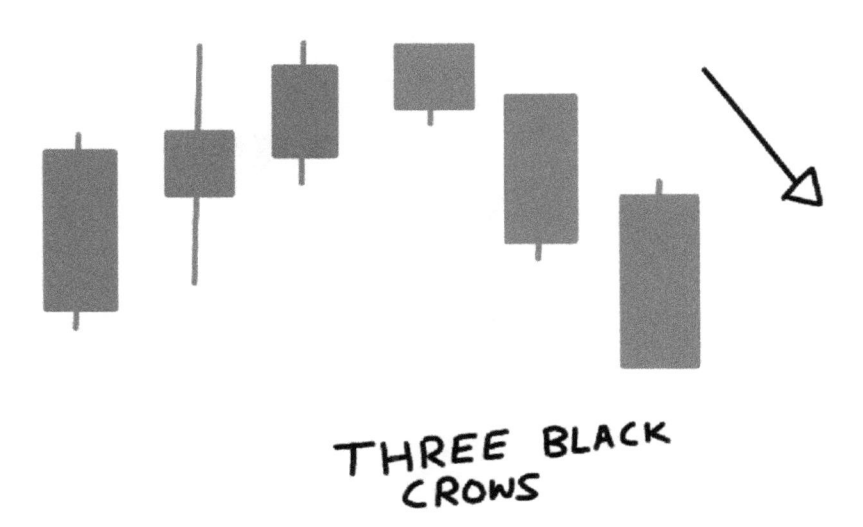

THREE BLACK CROWS

6. Dark Cloud Cover

This is a nasty one. Look for two long candlesticks, one green and one red (Or white and then black.) The red candlestick opens above the top of the green candlestick, but it closes well below - more than halfway down the green candlestick's body. It's not just balanced the upwards movement but exceeded it.

If the next candlestick doesn't come back up again, or if it only just manages to close in the very bottom part of the big red candle, then you have confirmation that the trend is going to be downwards.

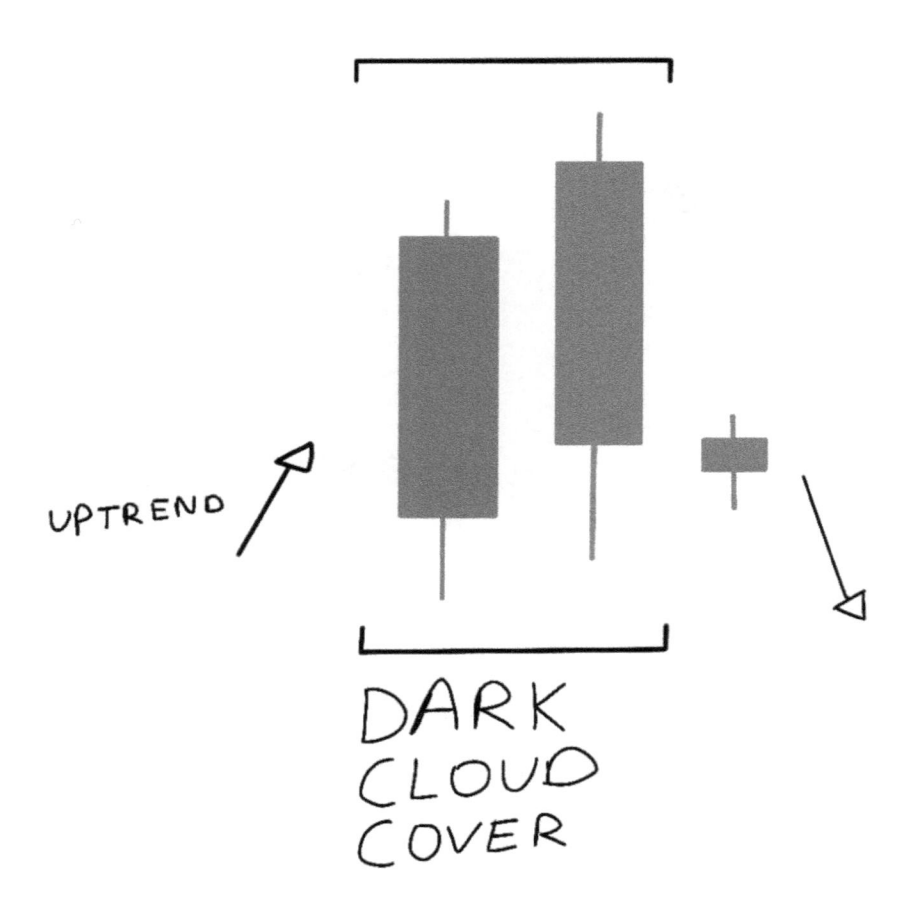

UPTREND

DARK CLOUD COVER

Four Continuation Candlestick Patterns

1. Doji

The doji is a funny little thing, like the 'star' in the evening and morning star; it's a candlestick that doesn't have much body at all, so it looks like a plus sign or a cross. A doji shows a day where the share price hardly changed at all.

While you find the doji sandwiched into the two 'star' patterns, on its own, it doesn't convey a signal; it's quite neutral unless it's in one of the other patterns.

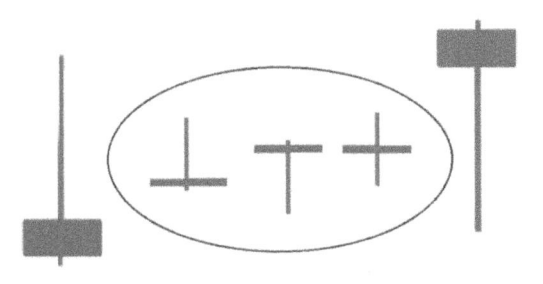

DOJI

2. Spinning Top

This is like a doji - a candlestick with hardly any body. But unlike the doji, it has really long shadows. That's why it's called a spinning top - it looks like a typical toy top.

Like a doji, on its own, it doesn't have a lot to say. With the spinning top, you can see that the price moved up and down a lot during the day, but closed not very far from where it started. So this could be a sign of consolidation, the market taking a breather, but things could go either way - down or up - once that period is over.

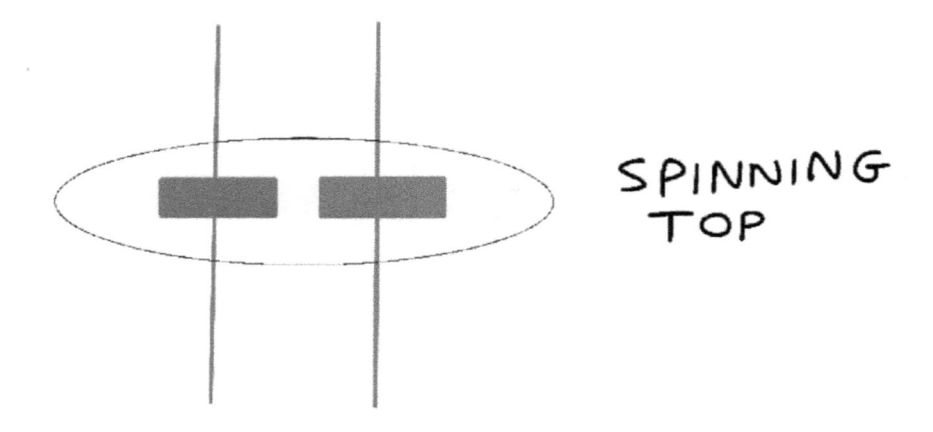

SPINNING TOP

3. Falling Three Method

Both the 'threes' are patterns that have three candlesticks of one color squashed in between two of the other color - green inside red or red inside green. In fact, you've got five candlesticks in all, so I don't know why it's not called "falling five".

Falling three has two great big red candlesticks on the outside. Inside, there are three, smaller, green candlesticks trying to break out upwards, but they fail, and the downtrend continues.

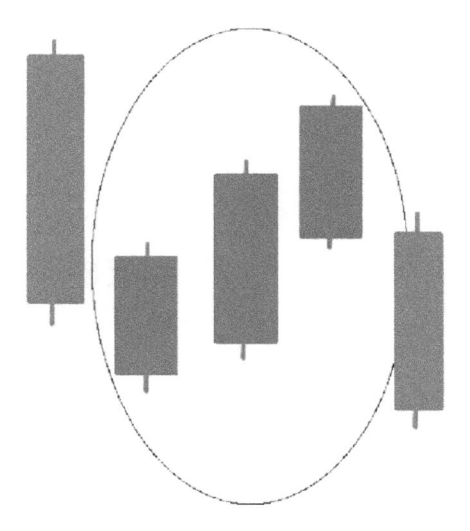

FALLING THREE METHOD

4. Rising Three Method

Rising three is just the other way around. Here, you have two big long green candlesticks on the outside, and three shorter red candlesticks are trying to break downwards on the inside. They don't manage it - the second green candlestick finishes higher than any of the preceding candles, including the first green one.

This is a good sign of an uptrend that's got a lot of strength in it and should stay intact for a good while.

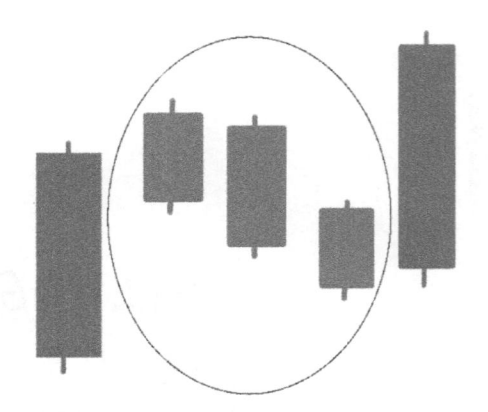

RISING THREE METHOD

And finally, the dreaded Marabozu!

The Marabozu is a particularly interesting candle since it has no wick or shadow at all. It's just a box. Either green or red.

That means the price did this;
- Green Marabozu - opened at its lowest and went all the way up to its high, where it closed.
- Red Marabozu - opened at its highest and kept falling all the way to the close.

So a Green Marabozu is a bullish sign, which can be either a continuation or a reversal signal depending on the trend. If it forms at the end of an uptrend, then the price will probably continue to go up; if it forms at the end of a downtrend, then a reversal is likely, with prices rebounding from their lows.

Conversely, the Red Marabozu is to be feared - it's a bearish signal. Avoid the curse of the Red Marabozu - unless of course, you engage in the black magic of shorting stocks!

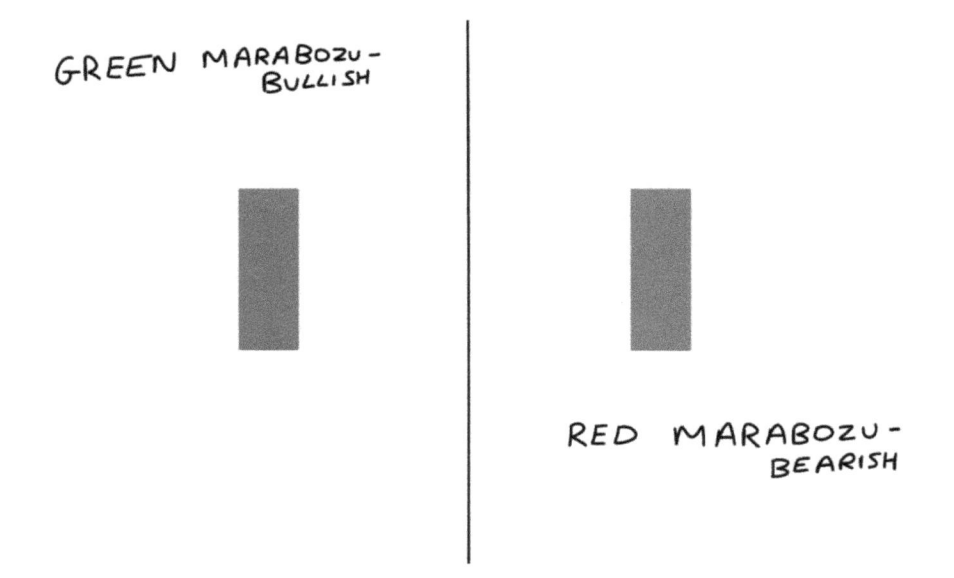

GREEN MARABOZU - BULLISH

RED MARABOZU - BEARISH

Let's just take a look at a practical example of candlesticks. Below is a chart for Oracle with what might be interesting candlestick patterns circled in blue. Can you see on 25th January and the day before, you've got those tweezer bottoms? The rise is very short term but it's definitely there!

Then at the beginning of March, you can see three white soldiers - although they're not, as they really should be, in a downtrend. Still there's a fast and furious rise just after them. (I think the gap down around 12th March was associated with a results announcement.)

Now there's another interesting series of candlesticks towards the end of the chart. Can you spot them? Which way would you trade?

It's another three white soldiers, I think. And I probably would be buying...

Chapter 7 Quiz

1. A candlestick's colored body shows
    - a) The high and low of the day
    - b) The open and close
    - c) The open and the high

2. What is a doji?
    - a) A candlestick with hardly any body
    - b) A very long red candlestick
    - c) A bearish signal

3. What is the opposite of Three White Soldiers?
    - a) Four White Soldiers
    - b) Marabozu
    - c) Three Black Crows

4. A candlestick that is colored red or black shows that the price
    - a) Went up on the day
    - b) Went down on the day
    - c) Did not move

5. Which of these are bullish signs?
    - a) Hammer
    - b) Inverse Hammer
    - c) Arnie Hammer

8

Chapter 8: Avoid the Traps

Trading chart patterns always sounds so easy to do. Websites show you successful trades that were profitable, and you look at the pattern and say, "oh yes, of course, anybody could have spotted that", and it looks so easy.

It's not. First of all, you have to kiss a lot of frogs - that is, for every chart that shows you a meaningful pattern, you're going to see an awful lot of charts where there's no clear trend at all. Secondly, some patterns can be deceptive and set traps for the unwary trader. For instance, 'headfakes' often happen when you were expecting a proper breakout. And thirdly... some traders make life awfully difficult for themselves, whether through being too emotional, not setting stop-losses, not considering risk, or not knowing what some of the *bad* patterns look like.

So in this chapter, we're going to take a look at some of the traps. And then in the next chapter, we'll look at trading psychology, and that includes a few more ways that many traders sabotage their own performance.

Fake-outs and Fake Head-and-Shoulders

Sometimes the set-up looks great... but then the expected price movement fails to emerge. Prices move the 'wrong' way for your trade. These are like a "headfake". But there are ways to check them out and avoid a few of the fakes.

You may fall into the trap of looking at a head and shoulders formation without realizing that it's actually just a blip in a bigger trend. Always check your chart with a longer time period before acting on a trade.

By the way, remember to check the pattern against the big picture. In the chart below, you think you see a head and shoulders formation, but actually, it's happening within a major trend and the trendline, not the neckline, is what matters. Always remember to look at several different time periods - I always look at a month, six months, a year and five years, which may be overdoing it - so you don't get caught by a pattern that doesn't work.

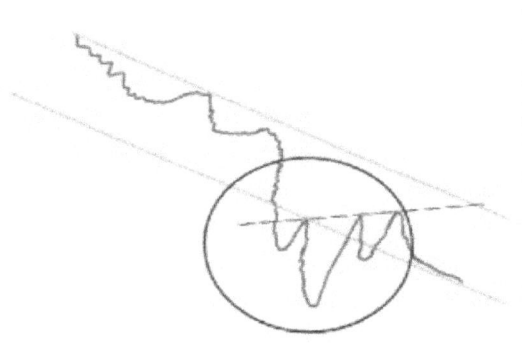

THIS LOOKS LIKE A HEAD & SHOULDERS BUT WHEN YOU LOOK AT THE BIG PICTURE ITS STILL IN A BIG DOWNTREND

Even if the price here had broken through the neckline, the top line of the downtrend channel would probably put up resistance, and that would limit your likely profits.

Or you may see the price come down to the neckline of the right shoulder, but not actually break through it. It might just dip below it in intra-day trading but still close above it. This isn't a proper breakout - wait for the price to close below the neckline before you buy.

In many head and shoulders patterns, there's a false breakout with a retracement before the real one. Sometimes, market practitioners are just trying to ensure traders with tight stop-losses are 'stopped out' before the price really moves. So don't put your stop too tight, and be ready even if it's activated to jump back into the next breakout.

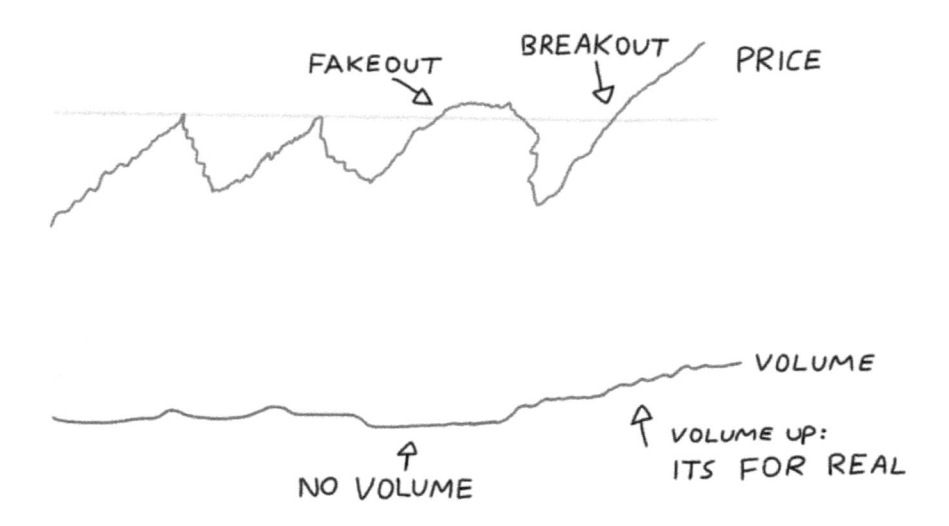

[Hand-drawn chart showing price action with labels "FAKEOUT", "BREAKOUT", "PRICE" on the upper line, and "VOLUME", "NO VOLUME", "VOLUME UP: ITS FOR REAL" on the lower line.]

You also get fake-outs - for example, the price breaks the trendline to the upside, but then it falls back again, instead of giving you the expected breakout. You'll probably fall into that trap a few times, but some confirmations can help you avoid it:

- If there's a low volume of trading, it's probably a fake-out; breakouts have high volume.
- If the price is headed very slowly towards the trendline, it's probably a fake-out; breakouts have real momentum and tend to start with a really big move.
- A fake-out from a double top or double bottom is one that doesn't lead to the expected reversal - instead, you get a continuation. If you recognize it, you can simply reverse your trade - if you expected a double top to lead to a fall, and the price starts heading up, then stop the short and go long.
- Try placing your stops just short of the 'expected' price or just a little more. Double bottoms, for instance, are well known patterns and lots of traders will have stop-losses at exactly the same price, often a round number. If you stay away from that level, you may not get faked out if the market-makers try to "shake the tree".

No Trend at All

Almost every good chart pattern needs a good strong trend established for it to work. It is really, really difficult to make money trading when there's no trend. And the market can be trendless for 60-70% of the time. If you don't trade for nearly three-quarters of the year, how on earth can you make money?

Mind you, if you don't see any good trades in a sideways market, don't force the issue. It's always better to have cash sitting in your account than to waste it trading for the sake of trading. Taking a risk when you haven't identified a return is one of the dumbest things you can do.

Mean-reversion trades are probably your best bet. The concept of mean reversion is that statistical probabilities group towards the mean (average), so that if a price goes to an extreme high, it will probably fall back; if it goes to an extreme low, it will probably rise again. Even sideways markets have a range, though they don't have a trend, so identify that range and you've got a trading strategy.

But to carry out these trades, you need to get four things right:
1. Detect oversold/overbought stocks using momentum and volume indicators, not just price charts.
2. Buy stocks when they are trading on the low side of the range. It may be profitable to wait for a slight bounce so you know you're not going to get stuck in a downwards breakout that could cost you money. Your target price is not the other side of the range, but the middle (so your profit is half the width of the range).
3. Be careful with your stop-losses. If there's a breakout, you do not want to get hit.
4. If there *is* a breakout, it may be worth joining it. Again, be careful; set a tight stop-loss.

You will not make big money in sideways markets. You can make a little. If markets are range-bound for a long time then you may need to consider trading them, but to be honest, the risk-reward ratio is not that good, so I prefer to sit them out. Or you might look at another market to trade - foreign exchange, commodity ETFs, or futures; but to do that, you really should have already at least paper-traded these markets, or you could be jumping out of the frying pan into the fire.

Adjust Your Moving Averages

Most chart packages have already decided which moving averages to display. These are often, for instance, the 9 and 18-day averages, or 9 and 26 day, or 50 and 200.

But these might not be the best averages for you. Don't fall into the trap of letting a charting site decide which moving averages you should use.

For instance, if you've decided to become a day trader, you'll want to get something like 5-8-13 bar averages. You can get price bars for every hour, every five minutes, or every minute even, so you might have a 5-8-13 minute average instead of 5-8-13 days. Watch out though, because though in a good trend, they'll give you great signals; in choppy trading, they can be all over the place, and you're best declaring time out, going flat (closing all your positions) and going to get a coffee.

If you trade longer term, you'll want to look at longer term averages such as the 26 and 50 day SMAs or EMAs. 20/21 are good for swing traders together with the 50 day; the 200 and 250 period MAs go well as the slower average.

Remember, the EMA moves faster than the SMA, so it will flag up trades more quickly - but you pay a price for this, because it will give you more false signals than the SMA. If you're happy making a lot of trades and closing the bad ones quickly, use the EMA, as it will get you into a price swing more quickly; but if you want to trade longer term, and keep your positions longer, then SMAs will give you winning trades that are slightly less profitable, but fewer stopped-out trades and fewer trades overall.

One of the reasons MAs work is that nearly everyone uses them. So while you might think it's fun to create a 34-day moving average, it might not give you any useful, actionable information. You can try it, backtest it on a few charts and see. But I doubt you'll actually find that it's a secret weapon. I've tried a few and they've never worked out.

And lastly, moving averages just don't work in trendless markets. When the market is ranging, don't try to use the MAs for trading ideas - they're going to be all over the place and will only get you into trouble. Wait till you can see a clear trend again.

Risky Symmetrical Triangle

We've looked at ascending and descending triangles, which can give you a great trading signal. But sometimes the trendlines form a symmetrical triangle. The highs are getting lower, and the lows are getting higher, and when the two lines meet, *something* has got to happen. The trouble with this formation is that it's super risky. The chances are 50% it'll be up, and 50% it'll be down, and at a guess about 90% that it'll be fast and furious.

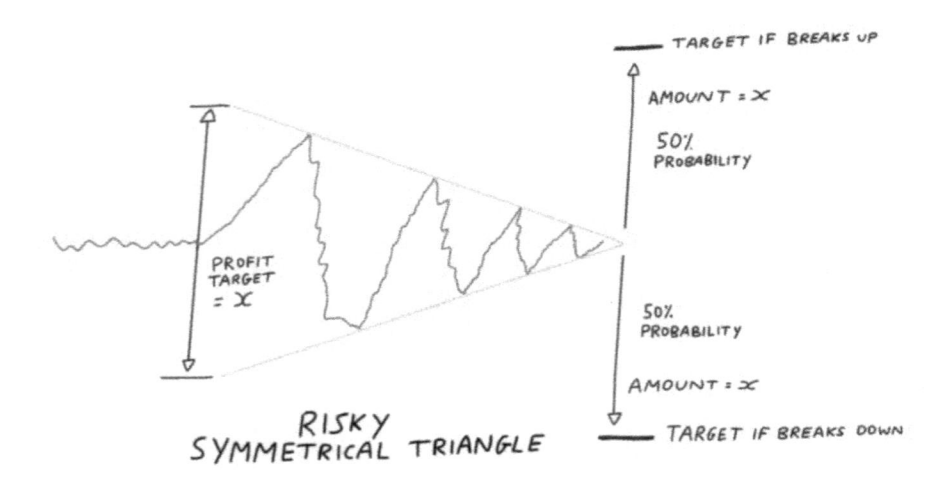

[Figure: Risky Symmetrical Triangle — Profit Target = x; Target if breaks up, Amount = x, 50% probability; Target if breaks down, Amount = x, 50% probability]

As I've stressed repeatedly, the trend is your friend, and trading a market that's not got a clear trend is tricky. And by definition, with one trendline going up and one coming down, with the symmetrical triangle, you have a trendless market - *unless* there's a really good strong moving average line, for instance, in which case you have a 50-60% chance that the breakout will be in the same direction. But there's also a good chance that there will be a fake-out first (usually with low volume while the real breakout will see an increase in trading volume).

So if you're risking on one of these triangles, it may be better to wait till the breakout and new trend is clear - and keep your stop-losses tight or the price could run away from you in the wrong direction. In fact, prices quite often gap up (or down) from these formations, so even your stop-loss may not help you.

Your profit target can be measured by taking the depth of the triangle when it began to form, and adding that to the breakout point. Your stop-loss should be at the last point at which the price touched the bottom line of the triangle. Since this is a 50-60% probable pattern, you're going to want a better than 2:1 risk/reward ratio for it to be potentially profitable. I wouldn't take it on much below 4:1, personally.

But you can ride the trend if you look at the moving average. As long as the price stays above the 20 or 50-day MA, you can keep your trade moving and bring your stop-loss up to date with the moving average every day. That way, you'll be stopped out automatically if the trend changes. A trailing stop like this is a great way to run a longer term position.

Super Rocket Stock

One of the big dreams of the stock market is the one stock that will make you your fortune. "If I'd put every penny in my IRA into this stock... if I'd mortgaged my house and bought this stock... If I'd maxed out my credit card to buy this stock..."

Point one: do not trade anything other than *risk capital*. That is money that you know you could afford to lose. If you lost your house and your pension, and owed the credit card company $50,000, you would be in dire straits. Don't go there.

But secondly, this dream is exactly that - a dream. Shares do not go up and up and up. They go all around the houses.

Let's look at Cisco - a 'rocket' of the tech boom. If you bought and held Cisco at $1.92 in 1994, you would have made a load of money. If you'd bought it at $15 towards the end of 1998, you would have seen it soar to over $80 - and then fall back to below the price you paid for it by the end of 2002. Now, it would be worth $50. (This chart's from Bigcharts. Their data goes way, way back. Not all chart sites have such good long term data.)

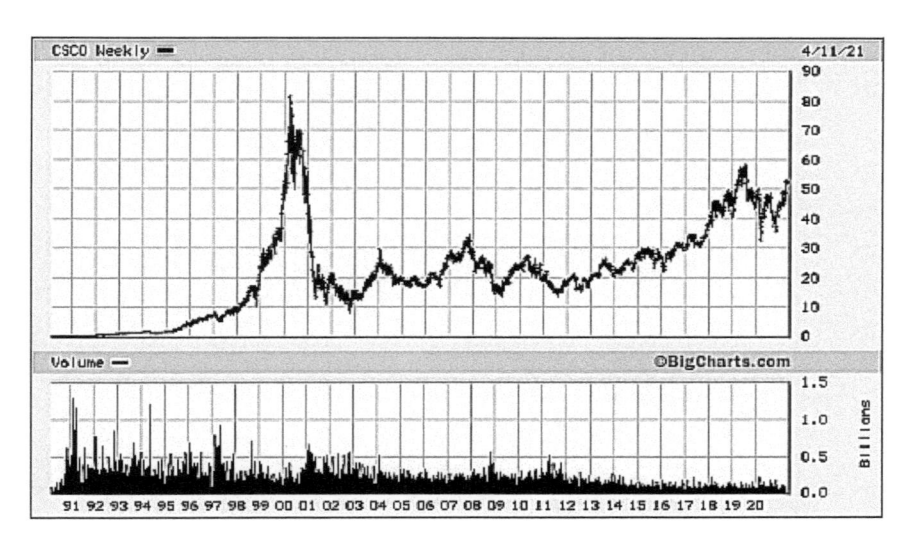

Plenty of gurus are keen to sell you their 'rocket stocks'. They'll use a combination of different approaches - analyst upgrades, earnings surprises, charting, trade volume. And they perform okay - for a while. But the problem with analyst upgrades is that analysts usually base their estimates on what the company tells them, and few analysts want to get out of step with a rising market - they fear if they call the top and the market keeps going up, they'll be fired. And the problem with 'rocket stocks' is that there are many other people who have got in at the same time, and the same price, as you. If things go wrong, they'll chicken out.

These stocks are often really speculative, like GameStop, for instance. I'd call Tesla a super-rocket - it's been driven by having a great story and a charismatic CEO, but it hardly makes any money, and competition from companies like Toyota, Volkswagen and Renault is heating up. (Incidentally, Volkswagen is up 62% from its lows. Good money for those who caught it.)

That means there's nothing to keep the share price from falling off a cliff. I know that we're talking about technical analysis and not fundamentals, but with stocks like this, I worry that the market is full of people who've heard the story but don't really understand the numbers. That pushes the stock up, and up, and up - and if you remember the parabolic rise? That's the trap.

Long Candles

In the chapter on candlesticks, we looked at several signals involving long candles. But sometimes, a super-long candlestick can be a trap. It looks like a bullish signal - and for a little while, it is. But while the share price may test resistance above this long candle, it's usually a bull trap and the share price will, after a while, come back to earth. And it can hit the ground hard.

Why does this big candle happen? New buyers are coming into the stock thinking that it's making a breakout. Maybe some big players are pushing the price up. What's important is that this long candle doesn't sit nicely among the other candlesticks - it's isolated. There may even be two big candlesticks.

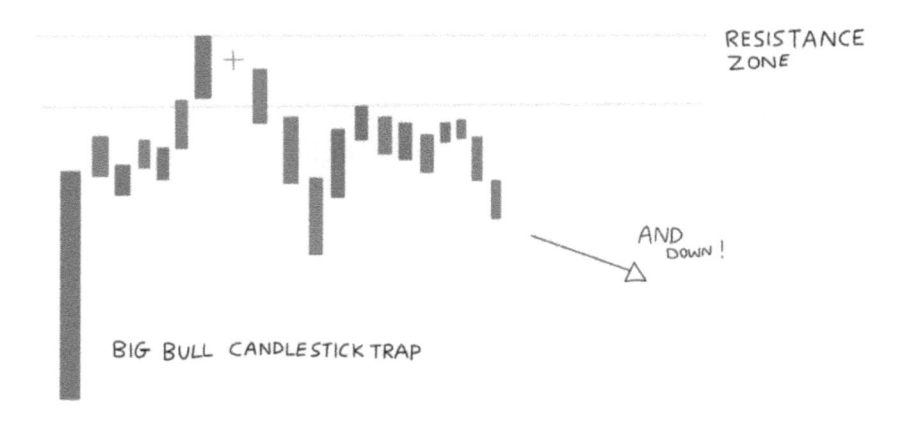

Maybe you missed that signal, and you're sitting in the trading range on top. You'll often get another chance, because a huge candlestick with a big upside shadow or wick will fake a breakout from the trading range. Novice traders will look at a big white or green candle and say, "Yay! Breakout!" Experienced traders will look at the big shadow on the upside, and they know that it means the market was trying to push prices higher and higher, but *it wasn't working*.

However, you should always check signals on a longer or shorter timeframe. For instance, a green/white weekly candle with a huge upper shadow looks as if the market tested the highs and couldn't sustain them. If you look at the daily candles, though, you may find that you have a pattern that is trading within the expected channel - up to the topside trendline and then just a small correction. In that case, don't get suckered - if you are long on the stock, it's still on course.

Lack of Discipline

The worst trap that most traders face is a lack of discipline. That might mean not getting up to catch the market open, not setting stop-losses, or not taking a trade where all the signals look good because you don't like the stock. Once you've decided on a trading strategy and on which signals are the ones you're going to trade, stick to your strategy and system. Chopping and changing loses trader's money…

… and that brings me to the next chapter, which is not technical, not about charts, and not about prices. It's about trading psychology - the psychology of other traders, but most importantly, your own.

P.S. Before we go onto trading psychology, if you are finding this book useful so far - I would really appreciate if you could spare 60 seconds and <u>write a brief review on Amazon</u> on how this book is helping you. It would mean the world to me to hear your feedback!

Chapter 8 Quiz

1. If you want to be a great trader, you have to kiss a lot of:
   a) Boys
   b) Girls
   c) Film stars
   d) Frogs

2. Three of these signs would tell you the 'breakout' is a 'fake-out', but which is the signal you can rely on to tell you a stock is going to break out upwards?
   a) The share price is moving slowly towards the resistance level,
   b) The share price goes above the resistance level in trading but closes below,
   c) The RSI looks overbought,
   d) The share price moves on big volume.

3. Rocket stocks are so called because
   a) They build space exploration equipment,
   b) They are rock solid,
   c) They are expected to go up like a rocket,
   d) Rocket rhymes with 'Reddit'.

4. How can you make money in sideways markets?
   a) Mean-reversion trades using oscillators,
   b) Head and shoulders formations,
   c) Candlestick charting,
   d) Shorting.

5. What is the worst problem which loses traders money?
   a) Worry,
   b) Lack of discipline,
   c) Setting stop-losses too tight,
   d) Not setting stop-losses tight enough.

A.Z Penn

9

Chapter 9: Trading Psychology

Trading isn't just about spotting the right chart patterns and making the right trades. It's also about what's going on in your own mind.

After all, the whole reason charting works is that it shows, in the aggregate, the sum of human behavior. Most of those humans will be prone to just the same emotions that you are - greed, fear, anxiety, excitement, doubt, and so on. But most of them don't make money trading.

In fact, statistics show that 80% of traders give up within a year. But then, 60% of new restaurants fail in their first year and 80% within 5 years, and you wouldn't think that was such a risky business as trading the market, would you?

So this chapter is about trading psychology, and mainly about you, and how you can stack the odds in your favor by understanding how the market tries to trigger a reaction, and how you can resist the reactions and emotions that will lose you money.

The Basics of Trading Psychology

I had a friend at university who was way, way better than me at math. He would have been a huge help to me when I started doing technical analysis. He could spot data patterns just from printed numbers - he didn't have to see a chart - and he came up with amazingly different ways of looking at common statistical problems.

Unfortunately, he got stressed out very easily. He flunked his first-year exams. He saw a psychologist, and the university said okay, fine, we understand, come back and we'll pretend it didn't happen. He just about managed through his second-year exams, with a lot of help from his friends, but when it came to finals, he just went missing. He couldn't even bear to turn up to the examination hall.

He didn't fail because he couldn't do the work. He didn't fail because he was stupid. He failed because he couldn't control his own fear.

He would never have made a trader.

If you are trading, you have to be able to overcome your emotions. The market can terrify you. During the tech crash in 2001, you could see some people were shell-shocked. They just couldn't think. Some of them panicked and sold everything. Some of them tried to put their heads in the sand and pretend it wasn't happening. Neither of these was a great strategy, though one or two of the people who sold did manage to get out of the market at a profit. They were too scared to think.

And the world is full of people who sat on massive paper profits for years. I had a friend who'd gone to work for a start-up, got shares in it, then it floated and she got shares, and they kept going up all the time, and she was a multi-millionaire… and then the tech crash came, and she was only 'just' a millionaire.

"Hey," I said, "I think you should sell your shares."

"You're joking! They were $152 last week and they're only $100 now; I'm going to wait till they hit $150 again and then I'll get out."

"They're not going to hit $150 again."

I could see her thinking that I was pretty good at this stock market stuff, and maybe it would be worth following my advice.

"What did you pay for them, anyway?"

"Nothing."

"Right, so you make a profit anyway."

"Yes, but they were $152. I just don't want to settle for less."

If I remember right, I convinced her to sell half of them. I hope she did. The share price kept going down all the way to single figures.

That's greed, and that's the second emotion that really ruins traders. (Plus, what she was doing was 'anchoring', which we will get to later and which is another thing that can really mess with your mind.) Greed can make you double up a position when your risk management rules are telling you that you're already running enough risk there. Greed can make you double down on a losing trade, lying to yourself that it's going to go back up. Greed can make you refuse to implement a stop-loss (which is why you should always enter a stop-limit order at the same time you make your initial trade).

To get back to charting, technical analysis can show you when other people are being greedy. Remember the parabolic rise? That's people getting greedy. It can show you when other people are getting fearful. Many breakdowns happen because people get scared as soon as they see their shares fall, and scramble to sell - and all the while the price is going down. Your edge is that if you can read the charts right, and stay unaffected by market panics, you can make money out of your trades.

So to be a successful trader, you need to neutralize fear and greed. There are several ways to do this.
- Zen: train yourself not to feel fear and greed.
- Discipline: feel fear and greed but then follow your trading system.

- Self-analysis: work out why you feel what you do about the market.

But in the end, you have to neutralize these emotions. That's what this chapter is about.

How to Get in The Mindset of a Successful Trader

Fear is a natural reaction. So is greed.
- You're crossing the street and a truck comes careering towards you. Fear says, "get out of the way!" And fear is right.
- You go out to a restaurant and just the wonderful aromas coming out of the kitchen make you feel hungry. Greed says, "Order *all* the dim sum!" Greed is right!

But these reactions are not necessarily good ones on the stock market. Let's do some thinking through them, and you need to do the thinking before you start trading, because once you're in the middle of the market, you're not going to have the time to think.

You have a losing trade. You've started with $1,000. You lose $25 or $50. What are you afraid of?
- "My first trade is a losing one; that shows I have no chance of ever winning." Hey, remember we looked at how your profit reflects the *profit potential* of each trade, multiplied by the *probability* of that trade being correct? You will *inevitably* lose some of your trades. It's a bummer that it's this one, but hey.
- "I was dumb to make that trade." No, you had good reasons to do it (well, I hope you did), but the stock market just moved the other way.

- "I'll lose all my money!" At $50 risk at a time, assuming you always use a stop-loss and you lose every trade and your stop-loss comes into play, you have to make 20 losing trades without winning a single one before you lose all your money. With only a $25 risk, you'd have to make 40 losing trades. This is what finance theorists call the risk of ruin - and this is why you have stop-losses.

There's another time people get scared. That's before they make their first trade. They sit on their hands. This would be right if the market is trendless, but otherwise, once you've identified a good trade, you need to make it.

- "I'm scared to make this trade." Have you looked at the chart? Is the signal clear? Did you get confirmation from another indicator? Have you identified your profit potential and your stop-loss? Is the money you're putting in less than 5% of your portfolio? So what do you have to be afraid of? Do it.
- "If I lose this trade, I'll lose my mojo." We already went through this.
- "But now it's for real." Er, yes, it is. Just remind yourself about the first time you did something you enjoy that felt a bit dangerous at the time - rock-climbing, surfing, playing a saxophone solo, whatever. For that matter, standing up and learning to walk!

Overcoming greed is actually easier because a lot of the time, your stop-losses will do it for you. If you set a trailing stop-loss for every trade, it will signal you when the price momentum has stalled and it's time to jump ship. Just obey the system. But you might also want to think:

- Do I need every single penny? If a stock goes from $408 to $525, but I'm only onboard from $415 to $501, does it matter? Or if I didn't get out at $525, and now it's $499 and my stop-loss is activated? I'm still making a lot of money. Not getting greedy is just about having *enough* on your plate.
- It's easier to make money when the move has momentum behind it. That means taking your profits out of the middle of a big trend is less risky than the profits at either end. Maybe not such a big profit, but a lot more bankable.

- There are thousands of stocks on the market. You'll do hundreds of trades, maybe thousands. This one doesn't have to make your fortune all on its own.

Now I will confess that when I'm on eBay and the minutes are ticking down on the auction for something I really want, my palms get sweaty and my heart beats a bit faster. But that's in my personal life. When I'm trading, I make my orders and that's it. So yes, you can *learn* to change your responses, and to take greed and fear out of the equation.

By the way, if you wanted to trade stocks because you think the stock market is exciting… please, don't. Using real money trades to prop up your ego or get an adrenaline rush is dumb. Take up an extreme sport instead; it's cheaper.

How Does Bias Affect Trading?

There are several kinds of biases that affect us when we make decisions. For instance, if as an investor I buy a stock, then a few weeks later I read that some famous investor bought into it or that Goldman Sachs issued a buy recommendation, really I ought to be asking, "Why did they do that? What are they expecting? Do they see the same value that I do, or is there something I missed?" Instead, I go, "Oh look, I made a good decision; other people are doing the same."

That's an example of *confirmation bias* - we notice and value information that confirms our existing beliefs. Sometimes we go a step further and indulge in *motivated reasoning,* which was described by Ted Seides in his book *Capital Allocators* as "confirmation bias on steroids". When we do this, we use our bias to argue against or discredit information that doesn't fit our views. The problem is, sometimes that information is right and we're wrong.

Commit yourself to look at and consider opposite views. When you're looking for confirmation of a trading idea in your second indicator, be tough - don't treat it as 'compliance', just ticking the box, but really have a good look and think about whether it really backs up the signal you think you've found. When you hear talk about a different way of looking for trades, or using different indicators, don't switch off and say 'That's not my way' - listen, question, think. It might still not be for you - but keep an open mind.

Representative bias is rather similar to confirmation bias. If you go to the Kentucky Derby twice, and both times you get the winner because you bet on a horse with a name beginning with B, does this mean the same strategy will work next time? But often, traders are inclined to copy trades that have been successful without thinking about *why* those trades were successful. So be careful not to get into this kind of lazy thinking; work out what you did right and *why* it worked.

Tribe identification can be a kind of bias that you don't even notice. You might say, "I'm a value investor", or "I'm a day trader." That ought to just be a description of your usual strategy, and perhaps it goes a bit deeper, if you've put some work into examining the philosophy of investing. But if it means you're trying to fit in with some idea of "being a day trader", particularly if you're part of a crowd on Reddit or Facebook and you're doing stuff that they do, because they do it - that's a bias. So is just blindly trusting gurus, whether they are called George Soros, William Eckhardt, Curtis Faith, Warren Buffett… or even A.Z Penn!

And then we have *hindsight bias* which is really a devil to deal with. Hindsight is always 20:20 vision, as they say; if a trade went wrong, it was the fault of the market, and if it went right, it was you being a trading genius. Keeping a detailed diary of *why* you traded as well as your trading records in cold hard cash is really important, both as a tool of education, and in keeping you clear of hindsight bias.

By the way, thinking in probabilities helps keep bias at bay. That's why I've stressed, all the way through the book, that you should have thought through the probability of a trade going the right way, the profit potential, *and* the risk that you are running.

If you make several losing trades, but all of them had a 70% chance of working out, and there's a 4:1 ratio between the profit potential and the risk - then you've only lost 4% of your total portfolio, you are doing things right. You had a streak of bad luck. Anybody can have a streak of bad luck. (In case you wondered how the 4% was calculated, it's $1,000/$50 x 20%).

On the other hand, if you tried to make the same trade you did last week, a stock that went from $40 to $50 and fell back to $40 so you're buying it again, without looking at whether the trendline has changed, what the moving averages are doing, whether the profit potential is still the same, and what the probability is this time around - you're doing things wrong, even if it works.

In the long term, discipline will win. In the short term, try to stay unbiased, and free from fear and greed.

7 Tips to Avoid Emotional Trading

1. Have good strong trading rules. Never take a trade that doesn't have the required profit/loss ratio. Put your stop-loss in place when you enter the trade. Know how long you are prepared to give a trade to work. Never bet the bank. Have the whole trade planned before you execute it.
2. Have patience. Wait for the right trade. There are 2,400 stocks on NYSE, 3,300 on Nasdaq, 832 on Euronext Paris, 2,483 on London, and that's before we talk about markets like Tokyo or the Australian or Canadian exchanges, currency trading, commodities, treasuries, corporate bonds, munis, or other instruments you could trade. There are enough trades out there in the world - you don't have to take a lousy one just because you haven't seen anything good today. Take a break instead.

3. Look after your personal life. If you have family, remember to spend time with them and not glued to the screen all the time. Participate in group activities and keep yourself physically active - do a sport, go out hiking with friends, whatever. Good traders do have addictive, obsessive personalities, so make sure that you don't let that side of you take over your entire life.
4. Plenty of traders like to be macho, but that's so last century. Look after your mind by doing breathing exercises, yoga, Tai-Chi, meditation or some similar calming and focusing exercise. It will help you keep your mind open and free from distractions, which is exactly what you need to spot trading patterns. Hey, there's even an app for all these!
5. Don't rationalize your losses ("it would have worked except that this happened"). Don't get angry. Don't think that losing means you're a bad trader; losing is part of the trader's life. Losing is not a judgment on you; your business plan accepts that you will have times when the market turns against you. You are not a fool for making that trade, it had the right ratios but the probabilities just didn't work out this time. You lost. Put it behind you. Get on with the rest of your life.
6. If you're feeling ill, or if you have a hangover, or if something else is on your mind (a break-up, an ill elderly parent or child, your tax return needs to be done) - don't trade. You will not be able to concentrate properly, and if you make bad trades while you are in this state, it's going to make things worse.
7. With any one trade, remember how much of your money is *not* in this trade. How much of your money is *not* at risk. Even if it sounds like a lot of money, remember that according to your trading rules, it's a tiny percentage of your total. Your lifestyle, your house, your entire net worth, is not at risk on this single trade.

And a bonus tip: FOMO is your enemy. Do not ever, ever let it get a hold of you. Fear Of Missing Out is not a valid reason to make a trade. It might be a valid reason to climb Kilimanjaro, visit Las Vegas, or do a parachute jump, but it's not a reason to trade.

How to Control Emotions While Trading

I'd like to quote a really successful trader, Victor Sperandeo, or 'Trader Vic'. In *Methods of a Wall Street Master*, he says: "When you make a trading decision, you should feel absolutely confident that you are right, but you must also recognize that the market can prove you wrong."

It's not easy. But remember that you are playing *probabilities*. You are making an educated and properly thought-through speculation, but things can happen that are outside your control. You cannot possibly know 100% of what's going on or predict 100% of the price movement, but if you know 80%, that's enough to be confident that you're making a good decision. But if the other 20% turns out to be different from what you expected, be flexible enough to change.

(A builder friend told me the way he thinks when he's looking for a renovation project. "I take a good look. Roof's good. Floor's good. No cracks in the walls. What needs doing? New electrics, new boiler, redecoration. Then I allow 20% for the fact that something's always going to go wrong." That could be the rotten floorboards that he couldn't see because they were hidden under a carpet, or the fact that the old wallpaper won't come off without wrecking the finish. That's not dissimilar to how traders think.)

Remember that every trade *is just one trade*. In your trading plan (which we talk about in Chapter 11), you actually expect a certain number of trades to fail. And you have an explicit rule against betting the bank. And you use stop-losses to get out of failing trades before they lose you too much money. So how bad is a single trade? It's an annoyance, but it isn't a wipe-out.

To get the emotion out of your system. Close the trade, then do whatever makes you feel better. For one trader I knew, he said throwing his telephone at the wall. He stopped doing that when smartphones got too expensive. Another trader I asked said, "Yeah, if I lose, I shout '**** you!!!!' at the screen. I know it's not logical and the market can't hear me, but it gets it out of my system."

Or you may not feel much emotion at all, in which case, close the trade, and get on looking for a better one right away.

Keep meticulous records - and a diary

You need to keep good records if you're a trader. First of all, at some point, the tax authorities are going to get interested in what you've been up to. Secondly, you need to be absolutely clear on your own risk position at all times.

But as well as just keeping your trading records, keep a trading diary. You should include the following sorts of information in it;

- How did you feel today? Tired, had a cold, felt great, a bit low on energy? Was there anything in particular on your mind?
- What trades did you look at and decide not to do? Why? (And to be a perfectionist, come back and see whether you were right to stay out, and note the details.)
- With the trades you committed to, what made you decide to do so? Did you have any niggling doubts or were you 100% certain? Did you get worried about them at any point? Were there any problems with execution?
- Did you get stopped out of any trades?
- Did you scale into any trades? Were you right?
- What was the market overall doing that day?
- What were the big headline items in the papers?

Looking back at that diary over a month can give you some good information. You traded a lot more shorts when you had a toothache, for instance. You missed some good head-and-shoulders trades, but you were right to turn down the channel trades. That tells you that you've got a good feel for head-and-shoulders, maybe do a little more work on those patterns and get more confident with them. You may find out you do better in a downtrend than you do in an uptrend.

As for the headlines - I find that sometimes 'Super Bowl = Kansas City Chiefs win' or 'Twitter suspends Donald Trump's Account' mean I can zero in on a day much more easily than if I just had the date. And sometimes ('Gulf War starts' or 'Brexit Referendum') the headlines will be one of the things that affected the markets.

I am glad I kept a diary because I had a quite aggressive medication for a bug that I'd caught for a few weeks a while back. After a week of trading, I looked at my diary. My trades were way out of line. I had one big winner and a whole load of bad trades, and a couple of bad trades where I had forgotten to put a stop-loss. I actually made money for the week, but it was clear that the medication had fogged my mind up. Until I finished the course of medication, I stayed away from the market. Without my diary, I might have kept trading - and I might not have been so lucky with the next couple of weeks.

Finally, analyze all your trades, particularly losing ones. Why did a trade go wrong? Did you miss something that you should have noticed? Perhaps you didn't check the volume indicators to confirm the price pattern, for instance. Did you break one of your trading rules? Did you set your stop-loss wrong? Was your order badly executed because you were trading an illiquid stock?

Analyzing your losing trades should teach you to trade better. It should also stop you feeling aggrieved or aggressive or depressed about losing trades - you know why you lost, so that's a mistake you're aware of and can learn from. And analyzing your wins? The same - why did it work? Did you take full advantage of the price movement? How can you make it easier to spot situations like that in the future?

Sticking to it

The real differences between someone who is going to win at trading and someone who is going to lose are very simple. The winner

1. Has a plan,
2. Puts the plan into effect,
3. Sticks to the plan,
4. and keeps going.

That's it. As you know if you've ever made New Year's Resolutions like "I will go to the gym," "I will not eat more than 1600 calories a day," "I will practice my guitar playing" … making the resolution is the easy bit. Sticking with it is the hard part.

Don't just learn the stuff in this book and make one or two trades. Have a plan for how many trades you're going to make, at what risk/reward level, with how much money. Don't just paper trade forever; when you understand what you're doing, make real trades with real money. And then keep going.

You might still fail. But if you don't do these four basic things, you have a 100% probability of failure. If you do them… you might actually succeed.

Chapter 9 Quiz

A slightly different form this time. Get a piece of paper and write down your answers.

1. How well do you handle fear? Think of some situations in the past when you've been afraid.

2. What New Year's Resolutions have you made and broken, or made and kept? Have you successfully changed a habit, like giving up smoking?

3. Do you make a lot of plans that you don't carry out? When was the last time you achieved something you had planned for a while?

4. Are you good at budgeting, doing things on time, getting your taxes filed? If not, what kind of difficulties are stopping you from being better?

5. Do you care more about being a success, or about other people seeing that you're a success? Why?

Have a good think about the answers. You may learn more than you expect, and the information could make you a much better trader.

10

Chapter 10: Ten Top Tips for Each Aspect of Trading

Ten Top Tips for Successful Technical Trading

1. Be selective. Only use indicators and patterns that you are really familiar with and used to using. Paper trade till you narrow down the indicators that work with you, and stick with them. Know what kind of stocks or indices you want to trade, and stick to them. If you want to introduce other markets or techniques, do the work, paper trade on them first, make sure you don't have too broad a focus.
2. Watch out for 'real world' events. Always know when Fed decisions, earnings releases, payroll numbers are coming out. If you think they will move the market, you can choose to go flat (close all your trades).
3. Don't rely on the naked eye. Just looking at the price chart is not TA. To do things properly, you need to know the patterns, you need to use the indicators, you need to draw trendlines. And that leads on to…
4. Always identify your profit and stop-loss levels and make sure the odds are stacked in your favor. Traders don't buy a stock "because it's going up" or "because it *will* go up", they buy a stock because they've identified a price point that it has a certain probability of achieving according to the patterns and trends they've identified. Plan every trade properly.

5. Protect your downside. "Scared money never wins" so never place a trade that could lose you more than 10% of your total capital. Use trailing stop-losses to protect winning positions that you've decided to let run. Use tight stop-losses on trades that could go against you.
6. Run your profits. Never close off a trade because it's in the money. If the trends are intact, then keep running your profits (and keep looking, never just trade and forget it). A good trader can make money with only a 40% win rate if all the winning trades return high profits. Use a trailing stop-loss to protect yourself, and if the risk gets high, take some money off the table, but run your profits.
7. Backtest your strategies, patterns, indicators, or at least test them by paper-trading for a while. Don't go straight into the market and trade. You can also refine your strategies and indicators - making quite small changes can have a big impact on the outturn.
8. Look at multiple time frames before you trade, so that you can identify the long term trend as well as the short term opportunity.
9. Have discipline. If your strategy is "buy every time the 50-day moving average crosses the 200 day, as long as the momentum indicator looks good", then do it every time. If you have a stop-loss, always use it. Don't overrule trades that fit your strategy because you have a 'feeling' about them.
10. Keep a journal. You can look back and see *why* you traded as well as what you traded and the outcome of the trade. Are you learning from your mistakes? Equally important - are you learning from your successes?

Bonus tip - keep learning, and keep refining your techniques. Sometimes markets change a little, and just tweaking your strategy can increase your profits. Sometimes a new indicator has advantages over the old version. Sometimes you'll read a book by one of the great traders and almost everything in it will be stuff you know, but you'll just get one piece of information that's new and that really makes a difference.

Ten Top Tips for Working with Indicators

1. Learn to recognize patterns. If that means printing out price charts and drawing all over them with a Sharpie - fine! Use a ruler and two different colored pencils. It's a bit subjective, so check up later whether your patterns worked out. If you just can't 'see' a particular pattern, concentrate on ones you can spot easily and that work for you.
2. Use trendlines, support and resistance. Again, if it means drawing on bits of paper, go ahead and do it; it will be worth it. These lines will tell you how much potential profit can be made, where to put your stop-loss, even - well ahead of time - where you might want to re-enter the trade.
3. Back-test or paper trade. Do this before you start trading, and do it if you ever want to introduce a new indicator or pattern, or try a different style of trading. Now, you may not be the kind of quantitative rocket scientist who's going to invent new indicators and tweaks and backtest them over 20 years of data, fine. But if you're not, at least spend a few weeks doing honest practice paper trading and making sure your new whatever-it-is works.
4. Don't run before you can walk. For instance, learn to read a candlestick chart, preferably by looking at a stock you know. Talk yourself through what's happening in each candlestick. Then what happened the next day. Then the next. Now look for the patterns - hanging man or shooting star or hammer. See where they worked and where they didn't. Get a feel for the charts. *After* that, you can start adding complexity.
5. Make sure that you know which indicators can actually give signals, and which are only for confirmation. If you expect the volume bar to tell you whether to buy or sell, you're never going to make money. Get a feeling for which confirmation indicators work best with the kind of signals you're using.
6. Use convergence and divergence. Often, an indicator's best signal is the fact that it's running *against* the price trend (divergence). Even just looking at volume - if the volume traded is falling but the price is still going up, there can't be many buyers left in the market. The day the last buyer has filled his or her boots, the price is going to look exposed.

7. Don't buy someone else's system. You're a human being and that means you are unique. If you make it as a trader, that uniqueness is your edge. Pick your own rules and your own indicators. If you like to make lots of small trades, don't go for a system built on following really big medium term trends, because it's never going to feel right.
8. Remember that no indicator will ever be right 100% of the time. This is where your trading record is important, because your % of winning trades and your % return with any indicator will dictate whether it's working for you or not. If it's only right half the time, but when it does it doubles your money, and when it doesn't, you're stopped out at a tiny loss, then it's worth using!
9. You don't need to understand how an indicator works (mathematically speaking) to be able to use it. I drive. I have no idea how my car works. I couldn't repair it myself, but I know how to drive it and that's enough for me. On the other hand, if I didn't know how the steering wheel worked, you're right; I'd be in trouble. If you have an indicator that you just can't get to work for you, then junk it.
10. Indicators come and go. Sometimes everyone wants to trade a new indicator and MACD is yesterday's news. But a bit like fashion, eventually, what goes around comes around.

Bonus tip: There is no secret 100% reliable indicator that will double your money every month with a single trade. Indicators like this exist only in the realm of marketing, and they are there to make someone else money - not you.

Ten Top Tips for Making Your Trades

1. Make sure you have a trading system and trading rules. These can be simple. In fact, it's best if they are as simple as you can make them. What signals do you trade on? What confirmations do you use? How much risk will you take with each position? How tight a stop-loss will you use? Write them down and make sure you can see them.
2. Get an online broker who is responsive and fast. Do some proper research and look at user reviews before you decide which to use. I have one broker who gets good prices but regularly takes fifteen minutes to fill an order; I only use it for investment, not for trading. It helps if your broker allows you to use stop-limit orders so you can set trades up to run automatically if the price hits your targets.
3. Many brokers have a demo system, so you can practice using the system to enter orders without putting your money at risk. It's worth using it extensively to make sure you understand the functionalities and any quirks it may have. If there's no demo system, it's best to start with a few small, simple trades rather than go wading in with a big and complicated set of orders.
4. Use limit orders to ensure you don't get put into a trade at the wrong price. If your trade had a profit expectation of $5, but you're put in $1 higher than you expected, you've lost 20% of your profit.
5. I've said this before, and I'm saying it again: ALWAYS set a stop-loss order at the same time you make your trade.
6. Don't trade stocks that are illiquid (have a low volume of trade), don't trade OTC stocks, don't trade stocks that have a widespread (i.e., the difference between the price you can buy at and the price you can sell at will take a bit of bite out of your capital). If you can't afford to trade round lots (100 shares), you may find it useful to use a broker that offers fractional trading.

7. Use a no-commission broker and make sure they don't have hidden charges. This will reduce the frictional cost on your trades.
8. Always check you have the right security and the right amount of shares. Double-check that it comes out at the amount of money you expected. Sometimes there will be two classes of stock for one company, or 'fat finger' has you getting quoted for 10,000 shares instead of 1,000, so always double-check before you confirm the order. (Don't ask me how I know this.)
9. Ensure your broker is regulated by your country's financial regulator. Check it out and make sure your money is secure with it. There are many sharks around - some very shady companies indeed, some of which make a habit of suddenly disappearing without a trace - particularly when it comes to non-stock assets like forex and commodities.
10. Make sure you have a laptop as well as your main computer, and a mobile (or a broker that uses a mobile app). If your main computer crashes, or your broadband provider has an outage, you're not going to lose your trading access or be stuck in a trade you wanted to get out of.

Bonus tip: choose a broker that doesn't have an account closure fee (or has a very low one). If you just can't get on with their order entry system, or if their service levels start to fall, you can make a quick exit without paying through the nose for it.

Ten Top Tips for Being Aware of Disruptors

The stock market *usually* follows its regular course depending on the laws of supply and demand, and the psychological probabilities of human behavior. But there are a few things you need to be aware of that can disrupt the usual price evolution of a stock and that can affect a market in ways you were not expecting. So watch out for these items on the financial calendar - and generally.

1. Corporate earnings releases. You *might* decide to trade the release because you have certain expectations - but you *need* to be aware that the results will be coming out on a particular day. If you're trading a stock, make sure you know the next results date.
2. Ex-dividend dates. When a stock pays a dividend, there is a particular date on which the shares go from trading *with* the right to receive that dividend, to trading *without* the right to receive it. The share price normally adjusts by the amount of the dividend. Again, be aware of the date!
3. Economic stats such as non-farm payroll figures, housing starts, and so on. This is one time that reading the financial pages pays off - because normally, they're not a big deal, but occasionally, the market is getting a bit worried about, say, housing starts, and if the number is the wrong one, the market can be spooked. So it pays to know if there's a particular focus on any one statistic.
4. Central bank announcements are always important, whether that's the regular Federal Reserve announcements, monthly Bank of England meetings, European Central Bank, or Bank of Japan - whichever of these markets you're trading. If you're trading ETFs, then you need to keep an eye out, as though individual stocks may be less affected, the broad index is likely to move.
5. Keep an eye on stock splits. Sometimes, chart packages fail to update, and it looks like the stock halved overnight - in fact, there's just twice as much stock in issue, and the system *should* eventually get round to showing it.

6. One wise trader once said the best way to trade the market is to look at the cover of all the magazines, and go short whatever's on the front. *Time* and *Newsweek* and *The Week* are all showing cryptocurrency headlines? Time to give up on Bitcoin! While that's not really a trading strategy, there's a grain of truth in it - avoid sectors that are being hyped.
7. Elections can move markets. However, they don't always move markets in the way all the experts say they will. Watch out for stocks that have a political sensitivity, though - for instance, with the increasing tensions between the US and China; I gave up trading Taiwan Semiconductor. I have better things to do than keep an eye on what's happening with US-Taiwan-China relations.
8. Personally, the moment I hear that a stock is the subject of takeover rumors, I stop trading it. The trouble is that technical trading works when 'all other things are equal', but if a bid comes way above the current share price, all trades are off. And if the bid doesn't come, that could see the share price tank. Some traders love this situation and believe the charts will show them what's going on, but my gut feeling? There are too many ways I can lose.
9. Okay, a slightly different kind of disruption. The week that stocks rallied after the big Coronavirus crash, Robinhood had an outage. If you only used that broker to trade, you couldn't take advantage of the bounce. If, on the other hand, you had a second account ready with, say, Fidelity, and enough funds in that account, you'd still have been able to trade. It's worth having two brokers just in case.
10. And as I mentioned in the tips for placing trades - make sure your own kit has redundancy. That is, if one computer or device goes down, you have another. If your cable, broadband and Starbucks Wi-Fi goes down, you have mobile data access.

Bonus tip: if you have a cat, do not leave your computer and keyboard unattended even for a moment in a room to which the cat currently has access. Don't ask me why. Just don't. A friend tells me the same is true for toddlers.

Chapter 10 Quiz

Ten top questions. There are no right answers, but there's time for a bit of self-reflection.

1. Why do you want to make money as a trader, instead of doing a job, writing a novel, becoming an entrepreneur, or investing long term?

2. What do you think is likely to be your worst fault as a trader?

3. What do you think you'll enjoy most about trading?

4. How much time are you planning to invest in your trading?

5. What markets do you want to trade? Why? (OK, I know it's cheating to have two questions.)

6. Have you already selected a broker or opened your brokerage account? If not, why not?

7. How will you make sure you're aware of disruptors?

8. How will you record your ideas and your trades?

9. What is your definition of success as a trader?

10. Exactly how much money could your cat cost you, and is it worth it?

I would just like to mention before we go onto the final chapter on Designing Your Trading Stategy, if you are finding this book useful so far — it would mean everything to me if you could spare just a few seconds and write a brief review on Amazon on how this book is helping you so far.

11

Chapter 11: Designing Your Trading Strategy

However good your recognition of patterns and your analysis of what's going to happen to the share price, you need to be able to execute trades successfully if you're going to make money. And you'll also need a trading strategy - an overall idea of how much risk you're taking, how much profit you ought to make for that level of risk, how many trades you need at what level of profitability and the probability to make your desired return.

It's basically a business plan. You'd expect anyone who's starting up a sandwich shop to have a good idea of how many sandwiches they're going to sell, how they're going to price them, what wastage they'll be left with, what their staff and rent costs are, and what profit they'll make. But a lot of traders get started without a business plan. They only have a few ingredients - hope, a bit of charting ability, and some money - and frankly, being a successful trader with those ingredients is like trying to make a sandwich with just ketchup, butter and mayo!

So in this chapter, let's talk about how you're going to set yourself up. What kind of charts you're going to look at, what kind of trades you want to do, the costs of doing business (yes, you'll have costs!), and how to work out your objectives.

Objective - turning $1,000 into $10,000

That sounds like a lot, but of course, that depends on how long you take to get there. If you left $1,000 in the bank at a 1% interest rate, you'd get there... in over 150 years. On the other hand, if you wanted to get to $10,000 in three months, you'd need to make a return of 23.3% on your money every week. That's not a lot, is it?

Okay, that *is* a lot, given the average return on the stock market is around 8% a *year*. But if you think about it, trying to make $1,000 into $1,233 in a week sounds less of a challenge than $1,000 into $10,000, doesn't it? (You might also like to know that Tony Sperandeo, in September 1982, grossed $880,000 on trading capital of $1 million - an 88% return in one month. He did have quite a few years of experience as a trader behind him at that point, though.)

You probably will take a bit longer than a few months to turn your initial $1,000 stake into $10,000. It might take you a year to get there. Meanwhile, if you'd left your money in the bank, you'd have $1,010 - ten bucks more than you started with. So okay, this is certainly an objective that's worthwhile, and that rewards the (controlled) risks you're going to take.

So the next thing is to think about your risk appetite. Because supposed to get from $1,000 to $10,000 over a year, you'd need to make around $750 a month ($750 x 12 = $9,000).

You could make that up in different ways:

1. With ten trades, of which only two win, but they make $375 each because you chose really strong breakouts (and tight stop-losses on the other trades), or
2. With ten trades of which fifty percent closed out at a small loss, and the other half made a bit more than $150 each.

Or, of course, any number of other combinations. For the sake of simplicity, by the way, I assumed you split your money into $100 stakes and only make one trade per stake. You might easily have traded more often than that. And in situation (1), with those two really strong breakouts, you probably should have scaled in on them, using what you had left from the losing positions to increase your winnings if the chart pattern showed the breakout was going to form a continuing uptrend.

Now that's just an example. You are going to have to think about how long you want to work to get there, how much time you have to give it every week, how often you're aiming to trade. But you'll be putting the numbers together that way - looking at how many trades you make, how many you win, what's your average win and average loss. That's basically your business plan.

But however great your risk appetite, **don't ever, ever bet the bank**. Divide your stake into at least ten lots of $100 each - some active traders work with an even more restrictive regime and never trade more than 5% of their money on a single trade. (However, they are willing to scale in - that is, if a trade is already profitable and the trend appears established enough to deliver a further profit, they might increase that stake, but only to a limited extent.)

Win rate/profit potential

Your success as a trader depends on two things; the first is your win rate (the number of winning trades as a percentage of all trades), and the second is the average amount you win (less the average amount you lose). That's how some people make money playing blackjack - they count the cards, work out the percentages, play a small amount for every losing hand and when they think the cards are coming out in their favor, make a much bigger bet. So they lose 90% of the time but make it all back in a couple of hands - at least, they do until the casino gets wise to it, and then it's time to call it a night.

Let's look at the win rate first. Technical trader Michael Masters claimed a 70% win rate, according to Jack Schrager in *Market Wizards*. No doubt you're hoping to claim that kind of a win rate. It would be easy to make money if you lose less than a third of the time, right?

But Vic Sperandeo, not a purely technical trader by any means, claimed that his win rate was only 40-50% - sometimes, he lost more often than he made money on a trade. And yet, he was regarded as one of the real Wall Street genius traders.

So although you need to know your win/loss ratio, that's only the first half of the equation.

Let's suppose your win rate is only 40%. You need to make sure that your wins make a lot more money than your losing trades lose. This is where your risk reduction rules come in. There are a number of factors here;

1. How much capital you place on any one trade,
2. The profit potential of a trade,
3. The loss potential of a trade.

Let's talk about (2) and (3) and how they relate to each other. I hope you noticed that when I talked about patterns, I often gave you the way to work out your profit potential.

It's systematic - draw those resistance and support lines, measure the depth of your triangles, count on the share price going exactly where the chart says it will. 'Hope' is not a word you're allowed to use - quantify the expected profit using the chart.

Now let's look where you need to place your stop-loss. Again you're going to do that by looking at the chart. And so now you have the expected share price, let's say, of a successful breakout, at $325, and if the breakout doesn't happen, you've placed your stop-loss just below the support line, at $285. You can buy the shares at $298.

So now you can work out your risk/reward ratio. This is where technical analysis really helps you. If you are a fundamental, long term investor, you *do not know* your risk/reward ratio; you can guess it, you can reduce risk by, for instance, buying established companies, which don't have too much debt and are unlikely to face major product liability lawsuits, but you can't quantify it. As a technical analyst, you can. You can measure the expected profit and the potential loss for every single pattern.

So for this trade: expected profit is $325 - $298 = $27, and the potential loss is $298 - $285 = $13. Your profit is twice as large as the loss, a 2:1 ratio. If you have a high win rate, you can be very profitable. But if you have a lower win rate, you need to be more demanding; the way Vic Sperandeo made his money was with a low win rate but an expected upside of 4 or 5 times the risk.

Remember that as a trader you need to think of the return on risk, not the return on capital. You may be buying $10,000 worth of stock, but if you have a stop-loss, that means you will sell out at $9,500, then you only have $500 of risk.

One thing is sure, though; if your risk-reward ratio is 1:1, that is, you're willing to lose a dollar for every dollar of potential profit, you are really unlikely to make a living trading! You would be surprised how many traders start off doing 1:1 trades, or even worse - usually because they are not actually working out the risk/reward ratio on their trades.

But how do I know my win rate?

Aha. You have guessed the problem.

Well, let's think of it this way. First of all, you have an idea, most likely, of whether you want to look for a few potentially highly profitable trades, or whether you want to be pretty continuously making small profits and turning your trades around. And you can also look at the probability of the types of trade you do - some patterns are more reliable, others have bigger breakouts but are likely to work out less often.

You still don't *know* your win rate. And that's why I'm going to suggest you should paper trade for a month first. I know, you want to get into the market and make your money... you're afraid of missing a profitable trade and a big uptrend... Remember, the trend is your friend, though, and FOMO is your enemy. Have patience and do your paper trading, find out your strengths and weaknesses, and most importantly, your risk/reward ratio. Then you've got a plan that, hopefully, is robust enough to withstand the worst the market can throw at it.

Changing the scale of your trades

Suppose you do exactly as we suggested and you turn your $1,000 into exactly $10,000. Will you still be making $100 trades?

I hope not. Because by the time you have a decent size portfolio of say, $100,000, you're going to be frazzled. There just won't be enough trades in the marketplace for you to make a return, and you'll be back to making the kind of money that passive buy-and-hold investors make. A mere 8% a year? Phooey!

Almost every successful trader changes the scale of their trades according to two factors;

1. The size of their trading portfolio,
2. Their form.

Obviously, by the time you've got a $10,000 portfolio, you should be placing $500 or $1,000 trades (depending on whether you want to move to the 10ths or 20ths of the portfolio). Scale up again every time your portfolio size doubles up. With a portfolio of nearly $2,000 you can make trades of $200, not just $100, and your risk profile per trade hasn't changed.

You should also change the scale of your trades according to your recent form. In particular, if you're making a typical number of losing trades, reduce your trade size. Randy Mackay, a hugely successful trader in the currency markets, was very careful about risk management. If you're losing, he always said, drop your size from 5-10% to 4% of your capital, or even 2% - make tiny trades till you get a winning streak again.

One trader quoted in Jack Schwager's *The New Market Wizards* even says that if he has three losing trades in a row, he calls "time out" and paper trades for a while till he feels his trading instincts are back on form.

He's actively engaging in risk reduction - minimizing the number of poor trades he's likely to make and maximizing the good ones. Sure, he's not making money while he paper trades, but he's not losing money, either.

So this is another element of your risk reduction plan. Think about what rules you want to put in place here. Above all, resist the temptation to make bigger trades when you have lost money, in the hope that you'll win it back. That's not how things work. Remember that you should always cut your losses and run your winnings - scale up your winners that are running strongly in a good trend, and chop your losers. The same applies to your form; trade a bit more money (don't get stupid!) when you're on winning form, and when you're doing poorly, stop yourself losing more money by trimming your trade size back.

Personal taste is important

There is no one size fits all rule. You may want to be able to trade full time within the next year. Or you may want to get started in a much gentler way, or to concentrate on longer term trades and only do maybe one or two trades a month. You may decide that you prefer fundamental analysis and investing in value stocks, but use what you've learned in this book to choose the best entry points and spot when the charts are warning you there may be trouble ahead. You won't make such fat returns, but if that's your style, you can still improve your investment.

Introspection pays dividends. Think about what you really want to do. Think about your strengths and weaknesses, think about how much time you have, think about your motivation. That should all feed into your trading plan.

What kind of trades?

While there are certain things that all good traders have in common, most will agree that to be a great trader, you need to find a way of trading that works for you.

For instance, what's your average holding period? For some traders, it's 3-4 weeks. For some, it's minutes. This might have to do with the hours you can commit to trading, but also, you may prefer to look at longer term charts and try to find major breakouts that can run for some time, and make fewer trades but with larger potential returns. Other traders like to make lots of small profits.

If you have a really mathematical turn of mind, you may want to trade options. If you are more of a visual person, and a lot of technical analysts are, you're probably happier trading the stock.

You may also, if you have a background in economics or you've been a fundamentals-driven investor before with success, find that a hybrid trade is your best trade. That is, you're already getting some ideas from the level of stock valuations or the way central banks are behaving, but while you allow that to suggest the kind of trade you should be looking for, you use TA to pull the trigger.

What kind of indicators?

You may also find certain indicators flag up trades instantly the moment you look at them, while others, no matter how much you try, don't make any sense at all. You should definitely *try* every kind of indicator and trade, but if you fall in love with candlesticks and they give you great, profitable trades with a very low failure rate, then stick with them.

But remember that as well as knowing how to get trading signals, you need to have a confirmation step in your trading rules. So if the candlesticks are giving you a hanging man, check the volume indicators and the moving averages just to make sure you're still happy with the trade.

And now… make your rules.

Making your Trading Rules

This is really important. Sometimes, if you're a successful trader, you'll just get a gut feel, "Hey, this market feels really trembly and on edge and it's overvalued, and I should really go short, because it's going to tip over and crash hard."

You might be right. You might be wrong. But you still don't bet the bank. You still apply your trading rules! That's why it's important to formulate good strong rules. Write them on a postcard, make them into your screensaver, have them on a post-it on top of your monitor, whatever you need to do. Here are mine:

1. Look for strong price signals: channel breakout, head-and-shoulders, good range trades. (I used to include Golden Cross, but it let me down once too often. Maybe I should give it another try, as that was a few years ago.)
2. Always confirm the price signal with another indicator (RSI or volume).
3. If in doubt check a third indicator. If that is not conclusive, don't trade.
4. Ensure the potential profit is at least 2x the stop-loss level, 3x or more if possible.
5. Trade in lots of [5% my portfolio size].
6. Place the stop-loss at the same time as the order.
7. Do not ever, ever break these rules. *The market can stay irrational longer than you can stay solvent.*
8. If you can't find a trade, don't try to make one.

(That bit in italics is a quote from John Maynard Keynes. Whatever you think of him as an economist, he was a genius market trader.)

Your rules could be a bit different. You might be less risk-averse than I am. You might use different indicators and look for different patterns. But they shouldn't be very different - and particularly not Rule 2, Rule 6, and Rule 7. They are the gold standard for traders. They will keep you in the game.

Because the one thing the rules *will* guarantee, if you get them right, is that you can stay in the game. That you will still have money to trade. That you won't lose the lot on one throw of the dice. And that when there is a profit to be made, you'll be there, at the right time, with some money to trade.

A word on being realistic

Many trading books and particularly trading gurus who sell seminars or advice lines will use words guaranteed to get your emotions racing. "Get rich quick," "Make a million," "How I made two million on Nasdaq," "Rags to riches." A lot of people think you'll only be a success as a trader if you are up there with George Soros - multi-billions and big, big calls like the bet he made against the Pound Sterling.

Well, maybe you do want to be a millionaire. But I wrote this book so you can start with $1,000 and have a chance of making a bit more. You may then want to go on and keep growing and growing and growing. You may say, "Okay, that was good, but I want to put some money aside"; one trader I know takes 20% of the winnings off the table at the end of the month and puts them in long term investments that he doesn't need to manage actively, like real estate or investment funds.

Or you may decide that while trading is great, you want to be able to take some time and bike Route 66 on a Harley, play with your kids, renovate an old house, or finish your Ph.D. One of the things a lot of very successful traders say is that they regret not having closer relationships with their children because they were too obsessed with the market.

So if your trading strategy is about just making your financial life a little better, and not about breaking out and becoming a multi-millionaire, *that's fine*. Don't ever feel guilty about it. You need to be disciplined as a trader, but that doesn't mean it has to be the only thing in your life - or that you need to be totally obsessed by it.

Me? When I'm not trading… I actually rather enjoy throwing dart arrows on my dart board. I'm never going to win the World Championship, but it doesn't stop me from having fun trying to get just that little bit more throwing accuracy out of the board!

STOP-LOSSES

Warren Buffett was once asked what were the rules for being a successful investor. He said: "Rule One: Don't lose money. Rule Two: See Rule One."

Chapter 11 Quiz

1. Your money at risk in a single trade is
    a) However much capital you invested
    b) The difference between potential profit and your stop-loss
    c) The difference between your money invested and your stop-loss.

2. Trading profit overall is created by
    a) Your win rate times your profit/loss per trade
    b) Your win rate times the amount you invest in each trade
    c) Being right 100% of the time

3. Who is responsible for making your trading rules?
    a) The Securities and Exchange Commission
    b) The writer of this book
    c) You

4. Which of these things should *not* affect the size of your trades?
    a) Your recent performance
    b) The fact that you really, really like this particular opportunity
    c) The amount of capital you have available

5. Which of these should you know before you execute a trade?
    a. The expected profit
    b. The stop-loss
    c. Both the expected profit and the stop-loss

6. Will you leave a review on Amazon?
    a) Yes, of course!
    b) Yes, I was thinking of doing it now!
    c) I'll think about it after I've finished reading.

Leave a 1-Click Review!

I would be incredible thankful if you could take just 60 seconds to write a brief review on Amazon, even if it's just a few sentences!

Amazon.com readers

http://www.amazon.com/review/create-review?&asin=B09B7B5W4N

Amazon.co.uk readers

http://www.amazon.co.uk/review/create-review?&asin=B09B7B5W4N

Conclusion

In this book, I've given you all the basics of good technical analysis. How to look at charts and spot patterns; how to draw trendlines, support and resistance lines; candlestick patterns; and how to use indicators like volume, stochastics and RSI.

The patterns are not always easy to see, but I hope I have given you enough examples both of the schematic way the patterns *ought* to look, and of real-world situations, that you have a good idea of what you're looking for. And while mathematical indicators like stochastics aren't all that easy to understand, once you start using them alongside other indicators and chart patterns, you'll soon see how they fit in.

But the most important chapters, I think, are those where I talk about psychology and about setting up your system. A good system will almost always beat a good trader without a system. And a system that you've created for yourself, that you understand and that suits your personality as a trader, will always beat anything that you can buy in the market.

I have to emphasize that even though turning $1,000 into $10,000 is a big ask; *you can do it*. Most traders fail for a number of reasons;

- They jump in before they're ready. They don't paper trade first.
- They don't understand how to evaluate the risk and reward ratio of the positions they take.
- They take positions that are far too large. If you do that, it only takes three or four bad trades to wipe you out. If you take limited risks, then even 20 or 40 losing trades will still leave you enough capital to stay in the game.
- They double down on losing positions. With technical trading, if a position is going the wrong way, it's very unlikely that it will reverse direction just to make you money. Instead, you need to concentrate on getting out of the trade as soon as it starts to go wrong, limiting your losses.
- They take tiny profits. If you're not winning a lot more than you're risking, then you only need a couple of losing trades and you're back in the red.

- They don't have a system. They chase reversal patterns one day, and they're following the moving averages the next, then they try Ichimoku, then they try candlesticks, then they try something else. Take time to find out the kind of signals that make sense to you, the patterns that you spot time and time again, and stick to the trades you know how to win.
- They let their emotions rather than their common sense drive their trading.
- After a couple of losing trades, they get despondent and give up.
- They think they don't have to put any work into the job.

These are all things you can do something about. Maybe you've read the book and you said to yourself, "That sounds really great ... but I can't see myself doing it."

Why not? Do you think you're not smart enough? Or do you not know how to work hard? Probably at the back of your head is a little voice saying 'You don't deserve to make money'. (I wonder where that comes from. A schoolteacher who thought you were dumb? Some kid in your class who wanted to rile you? An ex-boss you never got on with? It probably comes from way, way back - and you ought to stop listening to it!)

That's where the psychology comes in. You have to believe in yourself - you also have to be willing to say, "okay, I got this trade wrong". You have to treat your mind as one of the big assets of your trading business. If you run a big server farm, you'd want to make sure you maintain your equipment, keep the data servers cooled, and protect them from malware and viruses and intrusions. Treat your mind like that - keep it cool and calm, protect yourself from distractions and negative beliefs, and maintain your asset by occasionally reading a new investment book or looking up some new ways to trade.

The 90% of amateur traders who don't make money, or who don't make much money, are the ones who don't treat their brains as an asset. Don't fall into that trap.

Even if you looked at some of the psychology chapter and thought, "whoah, this is all a bit New Age", believe me - you don't need dreamcatchers and sacred crystals, but you do, absolutely, need to have a way of keeping your mind focused and calm.

You'll hear some people say that *no one* makes money out of trading. That is simply not true. You *can* trade using technical analysis and do well. Many traders use these techniques and make good money. You don't hear about all of them; some of them live a quiet life, don't get any publicity, don't want any publicity, but have a nice lifestyle and a good big pension fund thanks to their trading. Some blog or go on Reddit to boast about their best trades - and occasionally whine about their worst ones; you can take what they say with a pinch of salt!

One thing that's changed over the past 20 or 30 years has been the increasing use of computers in trading. Program trading shifts millions or even billions of dollars a day. But guess what? They're often using exactly the same kinds of mathematical patterns that we've looked at through charts and indicators. So if you're trading a breakout, you may well be trading a breakout along with a whole load of Goldman Sachs money or Morgan Stanley money - or hedge fund money.

And through sites like StockCharts, you can get access to huge amounts of data - just the same data that they have.

Add to that the fact that brokers like Robinhood offer free trading on stocks. You used to have to pay out minimum commissions of $40-50 a trade - and that together with the spread means there was significant 'slippage' in your deal. You needed to make over $100 just to cover these costs. Now, if you use an online broker, your costs are absolutely tiny - the spread on big stocks like Amazon is less than a third of 1% and in some cases, even less.

On some sites, like eToro, you can do 'social trading' - following traders with a recent good record. Some people do this in a lazy way, just replicating their trades.

I suggest you take a good look at their trades, as it's a great way to learn. You may learn that one style is definitely the best for you, or that there are some situations you don't feel very happy with, or you may see how not having the right stop-loss loses you stupid amounts of money - but if you go in with the right mindset, you'll learn.

You won't, of course, be starting with a huge amount of capital. But having a lot of capital is no guarantee of success; one joke going around Wall Street apparently is, "How do you make $2m from technical trading? Start with $30m in your hedge fund and just keep going." On the other hand, you'll be managing your risk, as I've shown you - my trading is a good deal more conservative than some hedge fund managers, as I don't use leverage (debt), I don't make big trades, and I have really, really tight stop-losses.

So get yourself started. If you have $1,000 as in our example, put that in as your initial capital. Keep it separate from your other money, and make sure it's money you could afford to lose. If you only have $500, start out with that. You could start with more... but to be honest, start small. When you feel more confident, you can add more capital to the business.

Paper trade for a while. If certain trades don't work out, go back to the relevant chapter and re-read it. Perhaps you misidentified a descending triangle which was actually a symmetrical triangle. Perhaps you didn't look for a confirmation from one of the momentum indicators. Work out why your trade didn't work (and remember that sometimes, they just don't).

Keep a tally of how each kind of trade performs for you - your win rate and your return on the trade. Trade the ones that do well for you and forget the other ones.

And when you're ready - make that first real trade with confidence and optimism.

May all your trades be good ones!

A.Z Penn

HOW TO GET THE MOST OUT OF THIS BOOK

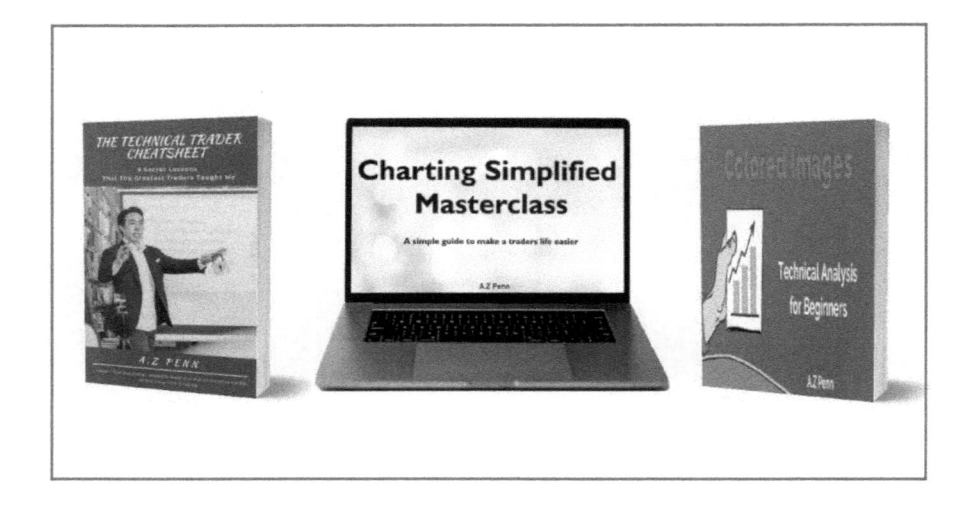

To help you along your trading journey, for this book in particular, I've created a free bonus companion masterclass which includes video analysis of real life stock examples to expand on some of the key topics discussed in this book. I also provide additional resources that will help you get the best possible result.

I highly recommend you sign up now to get the most out of this book. You can do that by visiting the link or scanning the QR code below:

www.az-penn.com

Free bonus #1: Charting Simplified Masterclass ($67 value)

In this 5 part video masterclass you'll be discovering various simple and easy to use strategies on making profitable trades. By showing you real life stock examples of a few charting indicators - you will be able to determine whether a stock is worth trading or not.

Free bonus #2: **The Technical Trader Cheatsheet ($12 value)**

In this cheatsheet you will be learning the 9 secret lessons that the greatest technical traders taught me. Believe me, when I started out, I thought I had everything set up to make a million on the stock market; but I was definitely in for a surprise.

Free bonus #3: Colored Images - Technical Analysis for Beginners

To keep our books at a reasonable price for you, we print in black & white. But here are all the images in full color.

All of these bonuses are 100% free, with no strings attached. You don't need to provide any personal details except your email address.

To get your bonuses, go to the link or QR code:

www.az-penn.com

A.Z Penn

Glossary

AI / machine learning - artificial intelligence and machine learning is giving a computer the ability to reprogram itself in the light of the information it has handled - basically, to learn. Computers can be taught to 'recognize' chart patterns and will then refine their definition of the pattern by the results.

Algorithm - an algorithm is a mathematical process, or set of rules to be followed in a calculation. Algorithmic trading uses a computer program that places trades according to the rules that have been set.

AMA - adaptive moving average: different types include KAMA, JAMA and HMA, after their inventors Kaufman, Jurik and Hull. For technical analysis, they work in a similar way to the normal moving averages and EMA.

Ascending Triangle - a formation where the highs and lows form a triangle with the point on the top edge. The price is expected to break out in an upwards direction.

ATR - Average True Range: average trading range, including the averaging out of all gaps.

Backtesting - running a test of a chart pattern against historical data to see how often a given trade rule would have been successful.

Bar - shows the open, high, low, and closing price (OHLC) of a stock for a given period in the form of a bar (high/low) with two 'tabs' showing the open and close.

Bear - someone who thinks the market or a stock will go down. They are 'bearish'; that word also describes a chart formation which is likely to lead to a downwards price move.

Behavioral economics - looking at economics as the sum total of individual actions, and bringing psychology to bear on why participants in an economic market behave the way they do.

Bollinger bands - bands that are placed one standard deviation above and below the moving average. They're useful because they show the volatility of the price - how much it's likely to swing.

Bond - a kind of security which pays a 'coupon' at a given rate of interest, issued by a government or corporate to raise debt funding.

Breakaway gap - a movement through support or resistance which is so strong that the stock 'gaps' through the line - that is, opening a trading session above resistance, or below support, leaving a 'gap' in the price chart.

Breakout - when a price breaks through a support or resistance line, or out of a chart pattern.
Bull - someone who thinks the stock market or a particular stock will go up. 'Bullish' might describe such a person, or a chart formation that suggests the price will go up.
Bull/bear ratio - a market indicator published each week that shows the number of advisors who are bullish against the number who are bearish.
Candlestick - an alternative to the bar, the candlestick draws a box between the opening and closing prices, with a 'wick' or 'shadow' to show the high and low of the trading session. It is colored white/green if the price went up, black/red if the price went down.
CBOE - Chicago Board Options Exchange, the largest US options exchange.
Chande momentum indicator - a technical indicator that uses momentum to identify relative strength or weakness in a market. Similar to the Stochastic indicator.
Channel - the band within which a stock is trading. In a typical chart, if the stock is trading in a horizontal range, you can draw one line joining all the 'tops' and one line joining all the 'bottoms', and this defines the channel.
Chart - a graphical representation of a stock's price movement.
Close - the closing price of a trading session.
Confirmation bias - when we believe more strongly things that happen to coincide with our existing beliefs.
Congestion - when a stock trades within a very narrow range of prices, showing that buyers and sellers are evenly balanced. It often happens after a major move in the share price.
Consolidation - a stock or security that is neither continuing nor reversing a larger price trend.
Continuation - when a chart pattern shows the share price should break out in the same direction as the existing trend.
Correction - when a share price falls because it has become overbought, but the overall uptrend is not broken.
Crossover line - when the price and an indicator (e.g., a moving average) or two indicators (e.g., two moving averages) cross each other.
Dead cat bounce - a sharp bounce within a major downtrend. Often, a market crash has a dead cat bounce that can look like a recovery but very quickly fails.

Death cross - when the 50-day moving average crosses below the 200-day MA. A bearish indicator.

Derivative - any security whose price depends on that of another security (e.g., an option, whose price depends on the underlying share).

Descending Triangle - a formation where the highs and lows form a triangle with the point at the bottom. The price is expected to break out in a downwards direction.

Dividend - some shares make a cash payment to their shareholders every quarter (usual in the USA), half-year (in UK), or sometimes, monthly. This is paid out of the company's profits and is called the dividend. Calculate the dividend as a percentage of the share price and you have the dividend *yield*, which you can compare with the bank interest rate - it's the money you will be paid on your investment. But of course, in the case of shares, the price can also move up or down, whereas the cash in your bank account, if you put $100 in, stays $100 - it's not going to turn into $50 or $125.

Donchian rule - buying when a stock reaches a four-week high and selling when it reaches a four-week low. The Donchian rule relies on momentum - the idea that if the stock has reached a four-week high it has established an uptrend which ought to continue.

Double bottom - a chart formation where the stock in a downtrend hits a support line twice and bounces off it both times; a breakout into an uptrend is likely.

Elliott Wave - the Elliott Wave principle attempts to identify long term 'waves' based on investor behavior, sometimes using the Fibonacci series.

EMA - Exponential Moving Average. This attempts to refine the ordinary Moving Average by giving more weight to more recent price moves.

ETF - An exchange traded fund, also known as a 'tracker', is a fund which replicates an index like the S&P500, Russell 1000 or Dow Jones Industrial Average. It's bought and sold like a normal stock, through a broker, and the big ETFs have tight spreads and low costs so they're a good way to trade the market.

Exhaustion gap - when a stock that has been rising fast gaps down. This shows that the price is no longer being driven by buyers - they are 'exhausted'.

False breakout / fake-out - when a share price crosses a resistance or support line, but then after a very small movement reverses the move. It's easy to fall into a trap here so make sure your stop-losses are good.

False signal - when a chart appears to be giving a signal, but in fact it's just 'noise'. You can help avoid false signals by checking the signal with a second indicator.

Flag - a short term rectangular trading channel running in the opposite direction to the main trend. You are looking for a signal when the price breaks out of the flag.

FTSE - the FTSE group runs a number of indexes, of which the best known is the FTSE 100, the UK stock market's biggest 100 stocks.

Fundamentals - the business realities behind the share, such as its earnings, assets, brand names, and operations.

Gap - when a share opens a trading session above or below the previous session's closing price, and leaves a gap visible on the chart. This can be a strong signal.

Golden cross - 50-day moving average crossing above the 200-day MA. This is a bullish signal.

Guerrilla trading - very short-term trading which aims for a low profit on each trade but making multiple trades within a trading session, often closing trades within just a few minutes.

Head and shoulders - a chart formation which forms three 'peaks' with the largest in the middle. It is generally completed by a breakdown from the third peak, signaled by the price closing below the 'neckline' joining the lowest prices in the series.

Heiken Ashi bar - Heiken Ashi takes candlesticks and uses an averaging formula to attempt to remove 'noise' from the chart, minimizing false signals.

HFT - high frequency trading, using computerized orders based on algorithms; can trade many times a second.

High - the highest price reached by a share during any particular formation. Also, 52-week highs, which are reported on financial news pages and websites.

Ichimoku indicators - this is a relatively new technique we have not covered, which attempts to forecast potential price ranges as 'clouds'. It's based on candlestick charting, but tries to extrapolate it forwards.

Index - a 'bundle' of shares created by mathematical means (e.g., the S&P 500). The index reflects the aggregate performance of all the component shares.

Indicator - an indicator is based on an arithmetic manipulation of the raw price data. Examples would be a moving average, RSI, stochastic or Price By Volume.

Island reversal - a candlestick pattern in which the stock price creates an 'island' top or bottom separated by gaps from the 'mainland' trends.

Kondratieff wave - Kondratieff waves are very, very long term waves. Personally, I am not willing to wait 40-60 years to see if my trades work out. Many academic economists don't believe in these waves, either.

Limit order - an order where you state a limit above which you are unwilling to buy, or below which you are unwilling to sell, a stock.

Linear regression line - the 'line of best fit' which allows all data points to be equally distributed around the line.

Liquidity - the ease with which a given security can be traded. More generally, the volume of trading in the stock market.

Long - to 'go long' is to buy and hold shares.

Low - the low point in any given price pattern or formation. 52-week lows can be informative and are found on financial websites alongside other basic price information.

MACD - Moving Average Convergence Divergence indicator. It shows the relationship between two moving averages, and can show changes in the momentum of the stock price.

Margin - if you trade on margin, you are borrowing money from your broker to buy the stock. I do not advise you do this. It is an easy way to ruin yourself.

Market indicators - these are used to forecast trends for the market as a whole, such as the market breadth index (the ratio between stocks which closed up, and stocks which closed down).

Market order - an order to buy stock 'at market', that is, at the best price your broker can get.

Market timing - trying to buy the market at the bottom and sell at the top. An impossible dream. Good traders are happy with getting 80% of the price action.

Maximum adverse excursion - the largest loss a single trade can suffer while it is open.

MBar or momentum bar (Constant Range Bar) - these charts, unlike conventional share price charts, do not show time. A bar is created for each move of a given amount, e.g., 10 cents. Some traders like these because they cut out a lot of 'noise'.

Mean reversion - the statistical likelihood that eventually extreme values will revert to the mean.

Momentum - the rate of change in prices.

NASDAQ - the second US stock exchange. It is all-electronic trading and has a higher percentage of tech stocks than the New York Stock Exchange.

Noise to signal - 'signal' is what we are looking for, something that tells us a stock is going to go up or down. 'Noise' is all the other stuff. It's like listening to old vinyl - the music is signal, the crackle and scratches are 'noise'.

NYSE - the New York Stock Exchange.

OBV - On Balance Volume, an indicator that shows up volume and down volume, giving a feel for how much of the trading volume relates to purchasers/bullish action and how much to sellers/bearish action.

Open - the share price at the opening of a trading session.

Option - a derivative that gives you the right to buy a share at a given price before a given date. It could simply be a private agreement, but most options are standardized and traded. Options are potentially useful because (1) they give you leverage, going up or down more than the share price, and (2) put options enable you to trade downtrends and breakdowns.

Oscillator - an indicator that shows values oscillating in a band between two extreme values, e.g., price acceleration between 0 and 100. RSI, Chaikin and ROC are all types of Oscillators.

Overbought / oversold - when a stock is 'overbought', all the buyers who are interested have already bought it, and it is exposed if any of them decide to sell. Indicators such as RSI and OBV attempt to show when stocks are overbought or oversold.

Pennant - a short term triangular formation within a defined up or downtrend. It is a continuation pattern, meaning that you'd expect to see the price break out in the same direction as the main trend.

Point-and-figure chart - these charts don't take account of the passage of time but create columns of price rises of a certain magnitude, reversing direction when the price direction changes. So if a stock price went up $10 every day for a week, and you had a $10 unit, you would end up with a column of five X's (or O's if the price were to go down). They are not much used these days, but the MBar is a more modern version of the same idea.

Put/call ratio - the proportion between put and call options purchased on a given day. It's a good way to measure whether the market is bearish (more puts) or bullish (more calls).

Pyramiding - involves adding to a winning position as the price moves in the desired direction. It can be a good way to make more profit from a really strong breakout, but the stop-loss for the whole position needs to be reassessed to take account of the higher average purchase price.

Quant - basically any individual in the investment community who bases their work on mathematics rather than gut feel, fundamentals, philosophy, or hype.

Range contraction - when the range within which the share price varies becomes smaller.

Range expansion - when the range within which the share price varies becomes larger.

Range trading - identifying the range within which the share price trades, and aiming to buy towards the bottom of the range and sell towards the top of it, again, and again, and again.

Resistance - the concept that a stock will have a certain price level that it has touched several times but never exceeded, and that this forms a 'resistance' to a move upwards. Drawing a resistance line is often a useful way of showing this.

Retracement - the amount that a stock 'gives back' from a rise (or fall) in the share price before the uptrend (or downtrend) resumes.

Reversal - a change in the overall share price trend.

Risk appetite / risk aversion - a trader's desire to take on more risk, or desire to avoid risk. Risk is a spectrum, and not all traders have the same appetite for risk.

Risk reward ratio - the ratio between the risk you run and the reward you expect. For an individual trade, the ratio between the profit target and the stop-loss.

RSI - Relative Strength Index. An oscillator that displays bullish and bearish price momentum.
Runaway gap - a gap in the direction of the trend, usually associated with high volume. A bullish indicator.
Security - any form of negotiable instrument representing financial value (e.g., a stock, bond, or option).
Share - a security entitling the holder to a share in the earnings and assets of a business.
Short - to 'go short' is to sell shares you do not own. You will consequently profit if the share price goes down, as you can 'cover your short' by buying the shares at a lower price.
Slippage - when your order is executed for a worse price than you expected.
SMA - Simple Moving Average. The average of the share price over the last x time periods.
Spike - a sudden and large move in the share price.
Spread - when you buy stocks you pay a higher price than you'd get if you sold - the difference is the 'spread' and its how market makers and specialists make their money. Spread is one of the costs you need to allow for as a trader.
Standard deviation - a measure of how far values differ from the mean. For instance, a class of ten-year-olds probably have a low standard deviation in height; they will all be roughly as tall as each other. SD is one way to measure the volatility of a share price.
Standard error channel - parallel lines drawn equidistant from the linear regression trend line to form a channel.
Stochastic Oscillator - an indicator which shows momentum based on the price history of the asset.
Stop-limit order - An order which specifies a price at which the order becomes valid, *and* a price limit after which it is no longer valid, e.g., "Sell 100 IBM *if* the stock price falls below 90 but *not* if it goes below 95." It's a good way of entering a breakout or breakdown trade.
Stop-loss - the price at which you will close a trade if it goes in the wrong direction. You should always set a stop-loss at the same time as you make your original trade.

Support - a line which the share price repeatedly hits and then bounces. If a stock falls, it will usually stop at the support line, either temporarily, or before returning to higher levels. If a stock falls through the support line, it may well fall all the way to the next support line.
Swing trader - traders are aiming to make gains by trading a stock and holding it just a few days. They almost always use technical analysis.
Technical analysis - reading patterns in the movement of the share price to ascertain the probability of the share price behaving in a particular way in future.
Tick bars - tick bars show price movement only if there has been a minimum number of trades.
Tracker - a fund that represents an index, that is automatically created and traded on a stock exchange in the same way as a share.
Trailing stop - a stop-loss that is increased as the price of the share goes up, so that you can't lose all your gains.
Trend - the general movement in a share price, either upwards, downwards, or sideways.
Trendline - a line that can be drawn to show the trend.
Triple top - where the share price forms three peaks all hitting the same resistance level. The third time, it is likely to break downwards.
VIX index - an index which measures share price volatility.
Volatility - the amount of change in a share price. A share price that tends to move 1% a day is much less volatile than one that swings by 5-10% some days.
Volume - the amount of shares traded on a single day.
Wedge - a chart formation in which the share price forms a wedge that is pointing up or down in the opposite direction to the trend. The price should break out in the direction of the trend.
Whipsaw - a sudden change in the direction of the share price. Sometimes a whipsaw happens before a real breakout, which can be deceptive.
WMA - weighted moving average.

A.Z Penn

References

There are a lot of books covering specific aspects of technical analysis if you want to go further.

If you're interested in candlesticks, Steve Nison has written several books on the subject which go into a lot more depth than I could here. He seems to know what he's doing, though personally, I find his mustache rather Ron Burgundy.

Jack Schrager's series of 'Market Wizards' books will not teach you technical analysis or trading - but they *will* give you a really good idea of how successful traders run their businesses. And they are very easy to read. What I particularly like is that Schrager does the interview, but then he sums up the learning points afterwards. My copies are well-thumbed because I'll always go back and read one of the chapters if I have some spare time.

John Murphy - Technical Analysis of the Financial Markets. If you want one big encyclopedic book with everything in it, this is as near as you'll get... apart from Tom Bulkowski's Encyclopaedia of Chart Patterns. One of the things I really like about Bulkowski is that he tells you the probability of each pattern making a successful trade - he's backtested all the patterns so his statistics are genuine. I can tell you I've made money out of this or that trade - but he has the math to prove it. He also shows loads and loads of examples (as does Steve Nison) so that you learn how to read a chart, and points out where common patterns sometimes *don't* work out so you know how to spot the signs if they're going wrong.

Curtis Faith's The Way of the Turtle is a great book particularly if you are undisciplined, a scatterbrain, or trade on 'gut feel'. He talks about learning to trade a system and learning to be cool with the results. I learned a lot from the book, not so much about technical analysis but about where I was going wrong not setting the right stop-losses, or picking and choosing my trades.

Martin Pring's Technical Analysis Explained is a lot of traders' basic book, and it's very comprehensive, but it was written in 1980 and to me, it does feel a bit like it.

Websites that are useful to anyone starting off technical trading include Investopedia: (www.investopedia.com/terms/t/technicalanalysis.asp), Slope of Hope (slopeofhope.com) which has good community functions so you can learn from other traders, and StockCharts' Chart School. And don't forget that if you trade with eToro (etoro.com) you have access to 'copy portfolio' and social trading features, so you can identify people who are performing well right now and follow them to work out what they're doing right. That's practically as good as the education you would have gotten sitting in an office with the old guy penciling those lines on the chart paper!

A.Z Penn

Quiz Answers

Chapter 1:
1. b
2. c
3. b
4. a
5. a & b

Chapter 2:
1. a
2. b
3. a
4. a
5. a

Chapter 3:
1. a
2. b
3. a
4. a
5. a

Chapter 4:
1. a
2. c
3. b
4. a
5. a

Chapter 5:
1. a
2. b
3. b
4. a
5. c

Chapter 6:
1. b
2. c
3. a
4. a
5. b

Chapter 7:
1. b
2. a
3. c
4. b
5. a

Chapter 8:
1. d
2. d
3. c
4. a
5. b

Chapter 11:
1. c
2. a
3. c
4. b
5. c
6. a & b

A.Z Penn

Ingram Content Group UK Ltd.
Milton Keynes UK
UKHW010809230623
423936UK00004B/146